Return on Engagement

Return on Engagement

Content Strategy and Web Design Techniques for Digital Marketing

SECOND EDITION

Tim Frick and Kate Eyler-Werve

Focal Press
Taylor & Francis Group

NEW YORK AND LONDON

First published 2010 by Focal Press

This edition published 2015
by Focal Press
70 Blanchard Road, Suite 402, Burlington, MA 01803

and by Focal Press
2 Park Square, Milton Park, Abingdon, Oxon OX14 4RN

Focal Press is an imprint of the Taylor & Francis Group, an informa business

Notices
Knowledge and best practice in this field are constantly changing. As new research and experience broaden our understanding, changes in research methods, professional practices, or medical treatment may become necessary.

Practitioners and researchers must always rely on their own experience and knowledge in evaluating and using any information, methods, compounds, or experiments described herein. In using such information or methods they should be mindful of their own safety and the safety of others, including parties for whom they have a professional responsibility.

Product or corporate names may be trademarks or registered trademarks, and are used only for identification and explanation without intent to infringe.

Library of Congress Cataloging-in-Publication Data
Frick, Tim.
Return on engagement : content strategy and web design techniques for digital marketing / Tim
    Frick and Kate Eyler-Werve. – Second edition.
        pages cm
    Includes bibliographical references and index.
  1. Internet marketing.   2. Social media–Marketing.   3. Strategic planning.   I. Eyler-Werve, Kate.   II. Title.
    HF5415.1265.F745   2014
    658.8'72—dc23   2013051221

ISBN: 978-0-415-84461-1 (pbk)
ISBN: 978-0-203-75181-7 (ebk)

Typeset in Minion Pro
by Apex CoVantage, LLC

Printed and bound in India by Replika Press Pvt. Ltd.

Contents

CHAPTER ONE

Digital Marketing Strategy Basics

We'll start and end this book with Climate Ride. This small, virtual organization, which produces multi-day endurance sporting events to raise money for environmental causes, has grown from an idea in 2008 to a vibrant fundraising community that has successfully used digital tools as a critical component of their growth strategy. With minimal resources, the co-founders set out to create a cycling event that could transform lives and raise money for a sustainable future.

Figure 1.1 Climate Ride's flagship event ends on the steps of the U.S. Capital, sending a clear message to politicians about the importance of environmentally-friendly legislation.

Just five years after the idea's inception, Climate Ride has granted over $1.5 million to their beneficiary organizations, which have a measurable impact on environmentally-friendly policy, nature conservation, triple bottom line business, bicycle and active transportation advocacy, and many other national programs committed to a sustainable future for people and planet. The organization has expanded their event offerings from a single multi-day cycling event from New York City to Washington, DC to similar events in California, the Midwest, and a five-day 50-mile hike through Glacier National Park, one of the areas in the United States hit hardest by climate change.

Climate Ride relies on its community of avid cyclists and environmentalists to fill their events and raise critically needed funds for these organizations. And they do so mostly through the strategic use of digital tools.

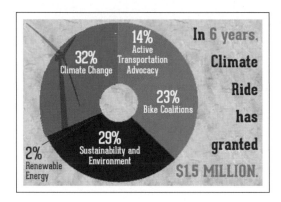

Figure 1.2 Climate Ride funds a sustainable future in several key areas.

Climate Ride co-founders Caeli Quinn and Geraldine Carter didn't have much of a marketing budget, but quickly found that digital tools like blogs, social media, online forums, photo sharing, mobile apps, and so on would play a key role in fundraising, outreach and organizational growth. Cost-effective with the "viral coefficient" potential to reach a vast audience very quickly, these tools and tactics are critical to Climate Ride's success.

The take-away here? With some knowledge, drive and resourcefulness, building a successful organization using primarily digital tools and strategy is within anyone's reach. Climate Ride is just one example of many that have done this.

It starts with a solid strategy: big picture stuff, setting tools aside and focusing on vision, mission and messaging. In this chapter, we'll define what it takes to create a successful strategy, then apply that strategy to multiple disciplines: marketing strategy, digital strategy, and content strategy. Then, we'll outline the steps you can take to begin building out your own organization's digital strategy. We will cover Climate Ride's digital strategy and execution of many tactics covered throughout the book in detail in the last chapter.

Defining Digital Marketing Strategy

The web is infinite, your budget and resources are not. A good digital marketing strategy should help you make decisions about how to use resources to achieve organizational goals on digital platforms.

A digital marketing strategy should do two things:

1. Clearly connect digital platform goals to organizational objectives.
2. Define success, so you can make data-based decisions about when to persevere and when to pivot.

Of course, "digital platforms" covers an ever-widening array of devices, services and channels, each one requiring specific skills and insights that often cross disciplines such as UX, content, development and marketing. As a result, two primary strategic challenges in the digital field are:

1. Integrating multiple disciplines, including content creation, user experience, web design, web development, analytics and marketing, into one coherent digital strategy.
2. Developing strategy-driven principles, guidelines, and goals that allow for flexibility and extensibility.

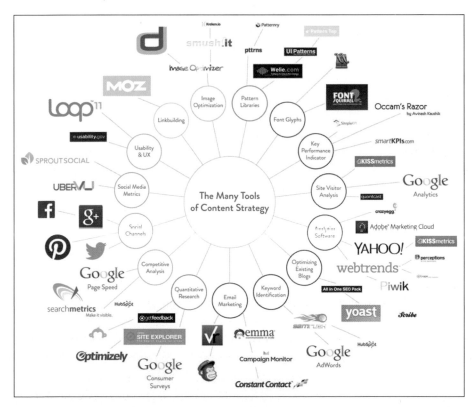

Figure 1.3 It's dangerous to go alone—take this book!

The Pointless Land Grab

Figure 1.4 CompassX Strategy founder Nancy Goldstein

Marketing strategist Nancy Goldstein owns CompassX Strategy, a certified Illinois B Corporation (more on B Corps later in this book) that creates sustainable growth for passionate companies. She advises that organizations be clear on their mission, message, and values before diving into digital. Here is Nancy's advice:

> Marketing is dead. Everyone says so. In fact, if you Google "marketing is dead," you will get 238,000,000 responses all saying that now, the only thing that matters is digital, keywords and engagement. To some extent, that is true. Companies can no longer talk at people regardless of whether they want to be talked at. Digital relevancy and engagement matter.
>
> But in the quest for digital relevancy and engagement as defined through keywords, likes and shares, many companies have lost their way. Without clear brand objectives, this quest is really just a pointless land grab. Just because you show up as the first result for a popular-but-not-yet-owned phrase doesn't necessarily mean it is right for your brand. Six hundred people liking or sharing your cat meme has little bearing on whether they will choose your brand or connect with you in a way that matters to you. Unless you are selling cat posters.

While digital marketing strategies will vary widely by organization, this book will lay out a set of foundational principles for understanding how to create a comprehensive digital marketing strategy that aligns with your organizational goals. We will also share a range of practical tips and tools to guide you through the process of developing and refining your digital marketing strategy.

Elements Of Digital Marketing Strategy

In this book we cover three key components of a digital marketing strategy: content strategy, design strategy and measurement strategy.

1. Content Strategy

Content Strategy requires identifying specific groups of users, developing key messages and content based on their needs and interests, creating content optimized for the channels they use and distributing that content at a velocity that maximizes its value to the user.

The goal is to develop content that is valuable to your audiences and deliver it where and when they need it. Content Strategy includes the following components:

- **Channel Strategy.** Channels are any platform you communicate through, including websites, apps, videos, emails, games, IVAS, and social media: Twitter, Facebook, and so on. The goal here is to figure out what channels will help you best tell your story to a targeted audience. Channels that are most relevant to your audience will obviously bring the most measurable success. In other words, don't open a Twitter account just because "everyone does"—have a plan.

- **Messaging Strategy.** Messaging strategy is the practice of creating custom messages geared at different target audiences.
- **Promotion Strategy.** Creating useful content is just half the battle—developing a strategy to promote your content tailored to each audience and channel will help you ensure that your content reaches your target audience.
- **Governance Strategy.** Governance and maintenance guides provide a structure to assess your content and resources, establish ownership and approval process, and ensure quality.
- **Community Building Strategy.** Targeting potential customers, oftentimes on social networks, who need what you offer and focus on maintaining regular, meaningful connections with them.

To ensure that the marketing actions you take are relevant to both your audience and your brand, consider the following questions:

- Does this action reflect how the audience you want to attract thinks about the product or service you offer?
- Does this action reflect how you want your brand to be known?
- What is the desired result of your audience engaging with this activity?
- How does it help you achieve your business goals?

Once you have answered these questions, your marketing efforts—digital or otherwise—will have more purpose and will be more likely to build your business in a meaningful way.

2. Design/User Experience Strategy

Designing for digital is designing for action: both the actions the user will take and the actions a site or app will offer in response to user input. In other words, user experience (UX) design is about how a site works *as well as* what it looks like. When business goals, content strategy, features and visual identity work in tandem the experience goes beyond utility to actual enjoyment.

Some core components critical to melding business and marketing goals with design/UX strategy:

- **User Research.** The first step in developing a successful strategy is to learn as much as you can about your audience. Market research (qualitative and quantitative), interviews, user personas, empathy maps and a range of other tools can help you get a solid picture of your core audience.
- **UX Tools.** The next step is to organize the data you gained from user research into actionable insights. Annotated site maps, wireframes and digital or paper prototypes, and other UX tools will help you map and test a compelling story.
- **Mobile First.** Nielsen reports that as of 2012, nearly 40%[1] of all web browsing is done on mobile devices. Following a "mobile first"

Sustainability and Accessibility

Though this isn't a book about either sustainability or accessibility, a website that meets present and future performance and energy efficiency standards while also providing an intuitive experience for users with disabilities will have a longer shelf life, reach more people, and show that your organization is mindful of a world beyond the customer conversion funnel. Plus, it's just the good thing to do. Here are some resources:

Sustainability

Check out Mightybytes' sustainable web design blog at http://mightybytes.com/sustyweb and author Pete Markiewicz' blog at http://sustainablevirtualdesign.wordpress.com/ for a plethora of resources on designing energy efficient, future-forward websites. For a quick resource guide, download James Christie's poster *Hack the Climate* here: http://bit.ly/19fThZG

Accessibility

508-compliance is the minimum standard to strive for when offering content for people with disabilities. Check out http://simplyaccessible.com/archives/ for tips on creating experiences that map to individual disabilities rather than just blanket support for screen readers. For basic 508-compliant tips, try http://bit.ly/c9h0eT.

strategy, which means developing websites for mobile devices first and adding styles as content viewports grow, will keep you ahead of the game to provide intuitive, rewarding experiences for users across the widest array of platforms and devices.

3. Measurement Strategy

One advantage of working in the digital space is the amount of quantitative and qualitative data at your fingertips. The challenge is making that data useful. Your measurement strategy should help you extract actionable insights from the sea of available data. Here are some of the things we'll cover:

- **Differentiating Between Engagement and Conversion.** Engagement is using digital tools to find, listen to, and mobilize a community around an idea. Conversion is taking action, like clicking an ad or purchasing a product.
- **Identifying Relevant Key Performance Indicators (KPIs), Targets, and Objectives.** Relevant performance metrics for both engagement and conversion track audience actions, like shares and purchases, rather than passive behaviors like visits and views.
- **Measuring Content Popularity and Performance.** Keeping track of things like traffic, bounce rate, and shares can give you insight into what types of content is attracting and engaging your audience versus what can be cut.
- **Measuring Design.** Digital analytics tools can measure the performance of web design elements, like image choices and calls to action.

The Mightybytes Content Strategy Framework

At Mightybytes, we have adapted and expanded a digital marketing metrics model originally created by Avinash Kaushik, former Digital Marketing Evangelist for Google,[2] to structure our thinking about content marketing strategy. Our framework solves for challenges at four stages of the content marketing development process: strategic planning, content creation, promotion, and analysis.

1. Strategic Planning: Getting buy-in

Planning around this framework builds a shared understanding across the team on:

- Defining "good performance"
- Choosing Key Performance Indicators
- The Process for analyzing metrics to produce actionable insights

2. Content Creation: Tying content to strategic goals

Our framework makes the links between strategy, content, and metrics explicit to:

- Provide a guide for writers, designers, and other content creators
- Make it easy for executives and managers to provide useful feedback

Figure 1.5 Use our Content Strategy Framework to get buy-in from all stakeholders when developing your strategy.

3. Promotion: Ensuring your target audience finds your content

Creating content is only half the battle; the other half is promoting it so that your target audience finds the useful and interesting work you've created for them. Planning for promotion in the strategy stage ensures that:

- Your content is optimized for your target promotion channels
- Your key performance indicators metrics are aligned with your promotion strategy

4. Analysis: Identifying actionable insights

Set the stage for effective analysis by choosing Key Performance Indicators, targets, and segments before you begin creating content. When the performance data comes in, you'll have a plan in place to make your two key decisions:

- What content/campaigns should we allocate more time and budget to?
- What content/campaigns should we cut?

Figure 1.6 Reference your Content Strategy Framework when creating content to ensure that you create content that aligns with your strategic goals.

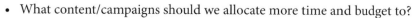

Figure 1.7 Establishing your performance criteria in advance makes it easier to make data-based decisions about what aspects of your content strategy to keep and what to change over time.

Content Strategy Framework Walkthrough

Feast your eyes on the framework in its natural state:

Name of the Organization	
1. Mission Statement	
2. Organizational Objectives	What the organization does to execute against its mission
3. Website Goals	What specific strategies you can pursue on your website or campaign to meet the organization's mission
4. Target Audience Goals	What your target audience comes to your site to learn or do
5. Content Hypothesis	What content supports both the website's goals and target audience goals
6. Promotion	How will people find this content?
7. Key Performance Indicators	Measures that help you understand if you are meeting your website goals
8. Targets	Pre-determined indicators of success or failure
9. Segments	A group of site visitors with a set of behaviors, sources or outcomes in common

Figure 1.8 The Mightybytes Content Strategy Framework.

Empty charts and columns aren't particularly user friendly, so in this section, we'll fill out the Content Strategy Framework as if we were an imaginary company, RoadshareChicago.org, planning out the strategy for a website redesign.

Roadshare Chicago is a non-profit organization that drives the creation of bike-specific traffic lanes by conducting research on the economic benefits of bike lanes and organizing campaigns to support bike lane legislation. If Roadshare Chicago was developing their website's content strategy, this is how they would fill in the framework.

1. Mission Statement

We begin with the organization's mission statement. We include this step for two reasons:

1. Beginning with the easy stuff is a nice warm up for the tougher work ahead, and
2. A mission statement can be vague, but objectives and goals must be specific and measurable. Creating a specific space for the mission statement makes it necessary to tease out organizational objectives and website/campaign goals later on.

We've created a splendid mission statement for our imaginary company, Roadshare Chicago:

RoadShare Chicago
We create healthy communities, healthy people and healthy business through bike lanes

Figure 1.9

2. Organizational Objectives

The first step in any strategy process is to identify what you hope to achieve. In the digital space, where content can be created with the click of a button, organizations can easily get distracted and waste effort, so it's important to tie every digital initiative back to organizational goals. After all, if your digital initiatives don't help you achieve organizational goals, then what's the point of pursuing them?

For example, if you sell a product, your site should increase sales. If you sell a service, your site should generate leads. If you are a nonprofit, your site should increase donations. If you run events, your site should increase registrations. And so on. Identifying these objectives will inform content, design, UX and measurement strategies.

Roadshare Chicago's three organizational objectives are:

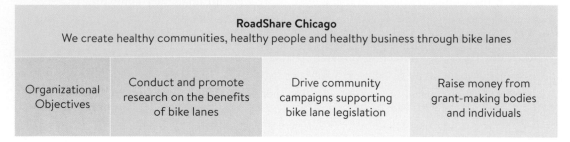

RoadShare Chicago We create healthy communities, healthy people and healthy business through bike lanes			
Organizational Objectives	Conduct and promote research on the benefits of bike lanes	Drive community campaigns supporting bike lane legislation	Raise money from grant-making bodies and individuals

Figure 1.10 What does your organization do to deliver against your mission?

3. Digital Platform Goals

Next, translate organizational goals into goals that can be achieved through the digital platform(s) you are developing a strategy for. The key here is to remember that your digital platforms are just one aspect of your organization. After all, a website will never be able to lobby a senator directly, a Facebook page can't deliver meals, and a Twitter account can't conduct investigative journalism. For the purposes of working on your digital platform strategy, identify goals for tasks the platform can do best. Drawing this distinction between organizational and digital platform goals is critical to keeping digital strategy in its proper place: in service of the overall organizational goals.

Digital platform goals are measurable, specific, and have a clear roadmap for improvement. Examples of some good digital platform goals include:

- Increase online donations
- Attract qualified sales leads
- Increase white paper downloads

For example, one of Roadshare Chicago's key organizational objectives is to conduct peer-reviewed research on the economic and social benefits of bike lanes. The organization devotes a great deal of time and money to conducting that research, but it all happens offline. Their website is used to *disseminate* that research. The final step in identifying your website goal is to identify your call to action, or the action you want your site visitor to take.

RoadShare Chicago We create healthy communities, healthy people and healthy business through bike lanes			
Organizational Objectives	Conduct and promote research on the benefits of bike lanes	Drive community campaigns supporting bike lane legislation	Raise money from grant-making bodies and individuals
Website Goals	Promote research Calls to action: download	Collect signatures for online petitions	Collect secure online donations

Figure 1.11 How can you best advance your organizational objectives through the digital platform you're strategizing about?

4. Align Target Audience Goals with Organizational Objectives

Now that you've identified digital platform goals, the next step is to identify the audience goals that overlap with organizational objectives. People come to your site for a reason: they want to learn something or buy something or do something. Conducting audience research, a topic we cover in great detail in Chapter 2, helps you identify your target audience's goals.

The key to an effective digital marketing strategy is to figure out the minimum content that will persuade your target audience to do business with you rather than a competitor. For example, your target audience might prefer a one-on-one training session, but would be satisfied with a video tutorial.

There is no one foolproof method for creating the perfect balance of audience and organizational goals. Get the right people on the project: content strategists to represent the needs and interests of your audience, marketing people to represent website business goals, and UX pros to flesh out how you can bring goals and design tasks together. These people will ensure that your target audience gets fair representation when setting business and marketing goals for website projects by including users in the process whenever possible through interviews, qualitative and quantitative research, human-tested prototypes, and so on.

In this section of the framework enter the results of the extensive work necessary to understand your target audience goals and tie them to your organizational goals. For Roadshare Chicago, the target audience goals that best overlap with their business goals are:

RoadShare Chicago We create healthy communities, healthy people and healthy business through bike lanes		
Organizational Objectives	Conduct and promote research on the benefits of bike lanes	Drive community campaigns supporting bike lane legislation	Raise money from grant-making bodies and individuals
Website Goals	Promote research Calls to action: download	Collect signatures for online petitions	Collect secure online donations
Target Audience Goals	Find research to inform/ support policy proposals	Take political action to promote bike lane legislation	Support biking in the community

Figure 1.12 What are the goals your target audience has that best overlap with your digital platform goals?

5. Content Hypothesis

This segment of the framework is your hypothesis about the content that you think will best persuade site visitors to take action.

We cover content strategy in great detail in Chapter 2, so we'll keep this section short! Roadshare Chicago's content hypotheses are:

RoadShare Chicago We create healthy communities, healthy people and healthy businesses through bike lanes			
Organizational Objectives	Conduct and promote research on the benefits of bike lanes	Drive community campaigns supporting bike lane legislation	Raise money from grant-making bodies and individuals
Website Goals	Promote research Calls to action: download	Collect signatures for online petitions	Collect secure online donations
Target Audience Goals	Find research to inform/ support policy proposals	Take political action to promote bike lane legislation	Support biking in the community
Content Hypothesis	White papers	Testimonials from community members/ businesses	Case studies on RoadShare Chicago's impact

Figure 1.13 What's your hypothesis about the content that will best meet both your business and visitor goals?

6. Promotion

Now that you've got a hypothesis about what kind of content will best meet your website and target audience goals, the next step is to decide how to promote that content so that your target audience can actually find it. The whole point of content strategy is to inspire your audience to take action, and the first step down that path is for your audience to actually find it! In this section of the model, it makes sense to list out your primary platforms, because you will use that information to determine your metrics of success. In our example, Roadshare Chicago promotes white papers primarily through email and testimonials through Facebook and Twitter.

Figure 1.14

RoadShare Chicago We create healthy communities, healthy people and healthy businesses through bike lanes			
Organizational Objectives	Conduct and promote research on the benefits of bike lanes	Drive community campaigns supporting bike lane legislation	Raise money from grant-making bodies and individuals
Website Goals	Promote research Calls to action: download	Collect signatures for online petitions	Collect secure online donations
Target Audience Goals	Find research to inform/support policy proposals	Take political action to promote bike lane legislation	Support biking in the community
Content Hypothesis	White papers	Testimonials from community members/businesses	Case studies on RoadShare Chicago's impact
Promotion	Email	Facebook and Twitter	Printed pieces, blog posts

Figure 1.15

7. Key Performance Indicators

KPIs, or key performance indicators, live up to their name: they indicate whether or not an initiative is succeeding in its goal. You can and should measure a range of things for your website and digital campaigns, but when planning your overall strategy, identify just one or two important, high-level KPIs. This doesn't mean you should stop measuring everything else. It just means you should be clear on your priorities. It is important to do this up front, as these indicators will inform many strategic decisions as you flesh out content strategy.

In their book *Lean Analytics*, authors Alistair Croll and Benjamin Yoskovitz extol the virtues of finding the *one metric that matters* (OMTM). Companies can measure dozens and dozens of metrics that will reveal performance insights, but at any given time in the life cycle of a business there is a singular metric that matters above all others. If you're just starting out, this might be generating awareness, so net increase in referral traffic from a specific source or likes on Facebook might be the OMTM. If you're further along in the business life cycle, referrals or churn rate—the rate at which users leave your site, close their accounts, etc.—during a given month might be most important to you.

We cover how to identify the best KPIs in Chapter 5, but here are Roadshare Chicago's:

RoadShare Chicago We create healthy communities, healthy people and healthy businesses through bike lanes		
Organizational Objectives	Conduct and promote research on the benefits of bike lanes	
Website Goals	Promote research	
Target Audience Goals	Find research to inform/support policy proposals	
Content Hypothesis	White papers	
Key Performance Indicators	# of links to each white papaer	# of downloads of each white papaer

RoadShare Chicago We create healthy communities, healthy people and healthy businesses through bike lanes		
Organizational Objectives	Drive community campaigns supporting bike lane legislation	
Website Goals	Collect signatures for online petitions	
Target Audience Goals	Take political action to promote bike lane legislation	
Content Hypothesis	Testimonials from community members/business	
Key Performance Indicators	# of people who sign each petition	% of visitors who sign each petition

RoadShare Chicago We create healthy communities, healthy people and healthy businesses through bike lanes	
Organizational Objectives	Raise money from grand-making bodies and individuals
Website Goals	Collect secure online donations
Target Audience Goals	Support biking in the community
Content Hypothesis	Case studies on RoadShare Chicago's impact
Key Performance Indicators	Average donation value

Figure 1.16 What metric best tells you if your content hypothesis is correct?

8. Targets

KPIs should be paired with targets and timeframes to set realistic expectations for steady, measurable improvement. Let's say that Roadshare Chicago's membership conversion rate for the past six months is 25%. Is that good or bad? If the target was 15%, it's terrific, but if the target was 60%, it's not.

The best way to set targets is to review historical performance and then establish a reasonable next step. If you don't have historical performance to fall back on, just pick a number that feels reasonable and give it a try. That may seem informal, but the reality is you have to start somewhere. Accumulating historical performance data will help you set more reasonable targets over time.

RoadShare Chicago We create healthy communities, healthy people and healthy businesses through bike lanes		
Organizational Objectives	Conduct and promote research on the benefits of bike lanes	
Website Goals	Promote research	
Target Audience Goals	Find research to inform/support policy proposals	
Content Hypothesis	White papers	
Key Performance Indicators	# of links to each white paper	# of downloads of each white paper
Targets	100 links within a month of publication; 500 within a year of publication	45

RoadShare Chicago We create healthy communities, healthy people and healthy businesses through bike lanes		
Organizational Objectives	Drive community campaigns supporting bike lane legislation	
Website Goals	Collect signatures for online petitions	
Target Audience Goals	Take political action to promote bike lane legislation	
Content Hypothesis	Testimonials from community members/businesses	
Key Performance Indicators	# of people who sign each petition	% of visitors who sign each petition
Targets	25,000	45%

Figure 1.17 Targets give you something to shoot for.

| RoadShare Chicago | |
We create healthy communities, healthy people and healthy businesses through bike lanes	
Organizational Objectives	Raise money from grand-making bodies and individuals
Website Goals	Collect secure online donations
Target Audience Goals	Support biking in the community
Content Hypothesis	Case studies on RoadShare Chicago's impact
Key Performance Indicators	Average donation value
Targets	$35

Figure 1.17 Continued

9. Data Segments

"Data segment" is a technical term used in analytics software to refer to a group of individuals that are similar in a specific, marketing related way. There are three basic segmentation categories:

- **Acquisition:** How do visitors get to your site? This includes paid ads, organic search, direct, social media, email marketing, etc.
- **Behaviors:** What are people doing on your site? This includes visiting pages and using any tools you provide.
- **Outcomes:** Are we reaching our conversion goals? This can range from signing up for a newsletter to purchasing a product.

Figure 1.18 Web analytics software services provide a range of default segments and options for creating custom segments. This is a screen shot of the Universal Analytics default segment/custom segment menu.

Segmenting your target audience into different groups helps you tailor messages to their needs and interests and then measure the performance of your tailored messages. We cover segmenting in more depth in Chapter 5. For Roadshare Chicago, the most useful segments are:

RoadShare Chicago Organizational Objective 1 Conduct and promote research on the benefits of bike lanes		
Website Goal	Promote research	
Target Audience Goal	Find research to inform/support policy proposals	
Content Hypothesis	White papers	
Key Performance Indicators	# of links to each white paper	# of downloads of each white paper
Targets	100 links within a month of publication; 500 within a year of publication	45
Segments	Traffic sources: Direct, ads, search, social, email	

RoadShare Chicago We create healthy communities, healthy people and healthy businesses through bike lanes		
Organizational Objective	Drive community campaigns supporting bike lane legislation	
Website Goals	Collect signatures for online petitions	
Target Audience Goals	Take political action to promote bike lane legislation	
Content Hypothesis	Testimonials from community members/business	
Key Performance Indicators	# of people who sign each petition	% of visitors who sign each petition
Targets	25,000	45%
Segments	New vs. returning signers	
	Traffic sources: Direct, ads, search, social, email	

Figure 1.19 What segment of our audience are we trying to reach with this piece of content?

RoadShare Chicago	
We create healthy communities, healthy people and healthy businesses through bike lanes	
Organizational Objectives	Raise money from grant-making bodies and individuals
Website Goals	Collect secure online donations
Target Audience Goals	Support biking in the community
Content Hypothesis	Case studies on RoadShare Chicago's impact
Key Performance Indicators	Average donation value
Targets	$35
Segments	First time vs. repeat donors
	Individual donors who contributed over $100

Figure 1.19 Continued

Using Your Content Strategy Framework

This framework is a working document. It's meant to be reviewed before creating content, used as a guide to configure your analytics software, and—most importantly—to make decisions about allocating money and time across all your digital efforts. To simplify things, create one framework for each digital platform you work on.

We spent a lot of time developing this framework to make it useful and actionable, but the truth is that what you put into the framework is less important than the act of engaging your organization in a structured conversation about strategy and performance.

Building out your Content Strategy Framework with your team and getting everyone's buy-in helps ensure that the decisions made based on your strategy will be understood and accepted. Funding issues in particular can cause emotions to run high, and pegging those decisions to KPIs demonstrates that decisions are based on data, not opinion.

Conclusion

In this chapter, we defined strategy types and introduced the Content Strategy Framework we'll be working with throughout this book.

What we discussed:

- Digital marketing strategy is geared towards creating opportunities for an organization to build deeper customer relationships on digital platforms.
- Digital Content Strategy is the practice of developing content that is valuable to your audiences and deliver it where and when they need it. The three primary elements of digital content strategy are content creation, user experience design, and measurement.
- Developing a strategy framework to guide content creation helps keep your content strategy tied to your organizational strategy.

Figure 1.20 Mike Volpe, CMO of Hubspot.

Profile

Mike Volpe
CMO, Hubspot, www.hubspot.com
Mike Volpe, Chief Marketing Officer of Hubspot, shares his thoughts below on inbound marketing, measurement and content iteration, marketing automation and more.

Mike leads the company's lead generation and branding strategy through inbound marketing, including blogging, search engine optimization, video marketing, and social media. You can read his articles and participate in webinars led by Mike at Hupsot.com and www. mikevolpe.com.

What has changed at HubSpot and in the market since the first edition of *Return on Engagement* in 2010?

Well, we've grown a lot! Today we have 10,000 customers around the world. We have 600 employees now and opened a European office in Dublin.

What has been the biggest change in the world of marketing measurement over the past few years?

More people are realizing they can measure most marketing efforts, and there is more and more interest in making marketing more scientific. I am not sure there has been enough effort at making measurement accessible to the mainstream marketer. Most marketing systems are still too complicated and require too much specialized expertise to implement and use them (except for HubSpot of course … ha!).

If there was one single measurement task, concept, idea that you think marketers should embrace what would it be?

I'll give you two. The first is do more inbound marketing.

Second, measure and iterate. You have more and more tools today to measure your marketing. You should not overthink things. So just try something and see if it works or not. Being fast and adaptive beats out careful and planned in today's fast paced world.

Why would marketers want to use a marketing automation system?

Marketing automation often makes it easier to send more and more spam to your email list.

What marketers should do instead is to figure out how to use inbound marketing to attract more prospects through SEO and social and blogging and then customize the buying experience through personalized interactions on the website, in social media and in email. This is why we built something different than traditional marketing automation at HubSpot.

What do you say to marketers who have concerns about automating what should be custom and personalized interactions with customers?

Only use automation to make interactions better and more personalized, for instance, using technology to enable your website to change based on who is visiting your website is a good use of "automation." Sending more emails to the list you purchased is not a good use of automation.

How are the terms "digital marketing," "content marketing," and "inbound marketing" different?

Digital marketing just means on the web, which can include banner ads and spam and crap that annoys people.

Content marketing is much better, it is usually less annoying to attract people to your business using content marketing techniques such as a blog and whitepapers.

Inbound marketing means transforming your marketing to attract people to you and interrupt them less—this includes content marketing but also encompasses free or freemium interactive tools or products (such as marketing.grader.com).

Where does content strategy fit into the above mix?

Content strategy is an aspect of inbound marketing. Knowing your customer persona well and creating content that they love is critical to making all this stuff work well.

How do you practice "lean marketing"?

We've blogged about agile marketing before. We're fans. We were also profiled in the Eric Ries' book *Lean Analytics*. In today's world, you need to respond to buyers and market trends quickly. The quarterly or annual campaign cycle does not match with how the world works. We try to come up with a game plan every month and then execute on that, then measure it, and then adjust to a better game plan the next month. Then repeat. We iterate toward success more than we do campaign planning toward success.

We've seen an increasing amount of overlap in shared disciplines between UX, design, marketing and content strategy recently. What advice would you have to web design firms wanting to build integrated teams with marketing, design, and development under one roof?

There is a ton of power in having more integration; it enables you to have fewer silos and have a customer experience that is closer to what the customer wants. It gets hard to do as you grow because you naturally need to break people down into smaller teams for management reasons, but try to organize your company according to the customer personas, not job functions.

What's your advice for someone wanting to incorporate A/B testing into their website marketing process?

Always be testing. There is no reason you should not just have a test running all the time—on your landing pages on your website on your email marketing. Look for a marketing system that has testing built in, not a separate testing system that has to be integrated with your other systems. That will make it easier to test more often.

Notes

1. Avinash Kaushik, "Nearly 40 Percent of Internet Time Now on Mobile Devices," Marketing Land, http://marketingland.com/report-nearly-40-percent-of-internet-time-now-on-mobile-devices-34639
2. Avinash Kaushik, "Occam's Razor," www.kaushik.net/avinash/digital-marketing-and-measurement-model/.

CHAPTER TWO

Content Strategy

Your content is by far the most critical component of your online presence. It drives traffic, informs users, builds awareness, converts customers, positions your company or people within your company as thought or industry leaders, as well as a slew of other things important to meeting strategic organizational goals.

People interact with your content to gain knowledge, learn a specific task or technique, find out more about you, read about your products or services, and decide whether or not they want to become a customer or part of your community. Search engines interpret your content and serve up pages in search results based on keyword use and a variety of other content-driven factors. Therefore, creating content that meets the needs of a targeted group of customers (or future customers) and is optimized for search engine "crawlability" will help the right folks find you and interact with your organization in a manner that, as long as you're adding value, potentially benefits everyone.

The single most common mistake organizations make is to start blogging and tweeting and so on without having a plan first. You need more than just words on a web page. Mapping out your organization's overall digital strategy in the first few rows of the Content Strategy Framework we covered in Chapter 1 establishes the foundations of that plan. In this chapter we'll focus specifically on content strategy, which helps you execute against the "content" hypothesis identified in your Content Strategy Framework.

What Is Content Strategy?

Author Kristina Halvorson defines content strategy as planning for the creation, delivery, and governance of useful digital content. Ultimately, content strategy addresses the key question that the new digital landscape prompts: with a zillion options for information and entertainment, how can I best reach potential

Figure 2.1 People are connected in more ways than ever.

customers and provide value to them? For starters, shift your mindset from thinking about what you want to say and start thinking about what your audience wants to know. Your potential customers are online for a reason. What are they looking for? What channels are they searching? What devices are they using? How can you reach them in a way that best suits their needs at a time or place when they need what you can offer?

Your goal is to figure out the answers to these questions so that you can develop content that is valuable to your audience and deliver it where and when they need it. Keep in mind that content isn't just copy or images. It's photography, audio, podcasts, blog posts, video, animations, games, emails—anything that you can use to relate a message or facilitate that self-discovery process.

Focusing on potential customer needs first doesn't mean you forget about business goals. On the contrary; it's a strategy for driving business goals. A good content strategy drives conversion and increases customer engagement by:

- **Enabling self-guided discovery:** Making it easy for potential customers to find the information, services and products they want at the right pace.
- **Meeting customers where they are:** Engaging your customers through all the channels they use for education and entertainment makes it easy for them to find you.
- **Tailoring messages to target audiences:** Creating key messages that groups of customers are most receptive to increases their positive sentiment and brand loyalty.

- **Maximizing impressions:** Publishing content at times and at a frequency that customers are most receptive to maximizes impressions and brand awareness.
- **Producing actionable results:** Getting measurable performance results enables you to adjust your content in real-time to maximize performance.

Creating Seductive, Compelling Content

The ultimate goal of developing a good content strategy is to create content so seductive that your audiences won't be able to resist reading, using and sharing it. That sets the bar pretty high. Still, good content strategy is all about engagement that meets goals:

- Creating content that people want to read or watch not only answers their questions but also improves their opinion of you.
- Creating content that people actually want to share increases brand exposure.
- Joining conversations about mutual interests with friends/followers is arguably more valuable than either of the above. Good content can drive those conversations.
- Creating content that increases conversions is just good business.

People in certain industries, especially those with technical or specialized audiences or those in highly competitive marketplaces, might argue that creating seductive, compelling content that cuts through the clutter and is useful to the reader is difficult to impossible. We disagree. While it may be tough, it starts with finding out all you can about your particular audience and providing them with the type of content that can only come from your organization.

First, think about the story you have to tell. How does your organization impact people's lives? Patagonia captures stories of adventures people have while wearing their gear:

Understanding Organizational Needs

If you are tasked with creating content strategy for a client you first need to understand their business. Here are some questions to help you better understand the organization you'll be working for:

Understanding Their Business

- How do they make money?
- What products or services are most profitable to the organization? Why?
- Is there a dedicated sales and/or marketing team, and if so, how are they structured?
- How is success measured?

Understanding Their Customers

- Who are the customers?
- What are their needs?
- How does the organization currently find (and keep) customers?
- Have user personas or other market research deliverables been created already? (If so, you need these.)

Other Relevant Questions

- What is the existing content creation process?
- Who approves content and how does that process work?
- Do editorial guidelines exist?
- Who decides what type of content to produce?
- What types of content does the team currently produce?
- What are the company's brand considerations?[1]

For a printable worksheet on identifying organizational needs, visit the *Return on Engagement* website at (www.returnonengagement.net)

Figure 2.2 There's nothing people love more than sharing photos of their vacations—particularly if they got to cuddle with a baby bear.

What value do you provide to your customers that they can't get anywhere else? MailChimp, an email marketing service with built-in survey features, analyzes the millions of surveys they deliver and reports on ways to make yours more useful:

Figure 2.3 Finding industry benchmarking information can be difficult and expensive. MailChimp makes it easy and free.

What can you share with customers that will help them make a decision about doing business with you? Chicago-based online community Threadless invites people to vote on which designs to print and sell:

Figure 2.4 Threadless invites their customers to decide which designs get printed, a terrific way to both boost community engagement and produce the shirts their most engaged customers want.

The chief stumbling block for companies is focusing on messaging that resonates with employees and owners instead of considering what will resonate with customers. For example, you may be very proud of your company's culture, but your culture isn't very interesting or compelling to customers unless you can show a clear connection between your culture and your service.

For example, Coyote Logistics helps companies move their freight as cheaply, efficiently, and quickly as possible. Their corporate culture prizes tenacious team players that get the job done no matter what. Their corporate culture story is directly tied to their customers' primary need: to get their products shipped, with no excuses.

Identifying your most compelling story is a key part of the audience research you will conduct when developing a content strategy.

Figure 2.5 Coyote's "no excuses" culture assures customers that they will receive top-notch service.

Conducting Audience Research

It is impossible to overstate the importance of audience research. You may *think* you know your customers, but without unbiased research, you may interpret their behaviors incorrectly. You (or someone in your organization) may have years of direct, personal contact with customers, but this doesn't equate to research that may reveal hidden information about why someone purchases your product or service over your competitor's. Audience research is important because it helps you prove hypotheses about your customers with actual data and actionable insights, which can result in measurable improvements to customer loyalty, brand awareness, and yes, the actual financial bottom line as well.

Swiffer, the house cleaning products purveyor, made a serious messaging error when they promoted their latest product, a steam cleaning mop, with an image of a woman dressed like Rosie the Riveter. Their target audience, women between the ages of 25 and 40, were incensed to see one of the most iconic images of working women used to shill for housekeeping products. The outcry was so immediate and pervasive that Swiffer pulled the ad, which meant that thousands of dollars and hundreds of working hours went down the drain, all for a lack of audience research and testing.

Figure 2.6 Research your target audience's likes, dislikes, and interests.

There are two primary approaches to audience research: qualitative and quantitative. Qualitative research is concerned with capturing insights and ideas from target customers (or users in the digital world); quantitative research focuses on identifying trends in data.

Qualitative Research

Qualitative research is generally conducted with a small, non-representative group of people. The goal is to create a loosely structured, objective environment that allows you to explore the thoughts and feelings of target users with the goal of identifying insights to improve your product or service. For digital content, qualitative research methods can include:

1. Conducting user interviews
2. Field observation of users
3. Automated user testing

1. User Interviews

User interviews can be as exhaustive as all-day focus groups with two-way mirrors or as simple as asking a few in-person questions. There are two primary categories of people to interview: existing and potential customers.

The specific wording of the interview questions will vary according to your specific product or service, but in general there are two categories of questions: what do people like and what are their pain points?

1. What do they like about your product or service? What would make them purchase, donate, or otherwise use your solution, find your content valuable, etc.?
2. What are their pain points? What are the roadblocks to purchase?

You can get much more detailed than the above questions, but try to keep your interview specific and focused to provide insights that are actionable. For a list of user interview questions and an editable interview handout, visit the *Return on Engagement* website at www.returnonengagement.net.

2. Field Observations of Users

Sometimes the most useful results come from just sitting back and watching a customer try to accomplish a task, like commenting on a blog post, registering for an event, etc. Designers can use affordable online meeting tools like Skype or GoToMeeting to watch how a customer moves through a website. You can ask the same types of questions you might ask in a field observation. The benefit of remote testing is that you can conduct quick tests at every stage of the development cycle. This can be particularly helpful in an agile web development process, where small changes to a site's design are rolled out very quickly and frequently.

3. Automated User Testing

Designers can also use specialized but affordable usability testing tools, such as www.loop11.com, which automatically gathers customer feedback and records their behavior. The benefit to this approach is to replicate traditional usability testing techniques, which strive to gather a customer's feedback without influencing their behavior or responses.

You should definitely poll more than just one or two users (or potential users), but keep it manageable. The purpose of qualitative research is right in the name. Use it to glean useful insights from people who are exemplary of those you wish to reach with your content, product, or service. For data trends across a wide number of users, you'll want to use quantitative analysis.

Quantitative Audience Research

Quantitative analysis provides trend data through numbers. Research results are typically anonymous and answers are candid. Two simple options for conducting quantitative user research are:

1. Analyzing site visitor metrics
2. Conducting audience surveys

1. Site Visitor Analysis

While it's great to survey your audience to get their candid feedback on usability, intentions, and satisfaction, it's always a good idea to round out your research with unfiltered data that comes from analytics tools. A wide range of tools exist to help you gather quantitative data on site visitors. This data can help you create a more accurate picture of your audience by providing detail like geographic location, demographic information, and what specific actions visitors are taking on your website. We like:

- **Quantcast.** A free tool that captures demographic information about your visitors.
- **Universal Analytics.** A free tool that captures a wealth of information about how visitors find your site and what they do when they get there.
- **KissMetrics.** A paid service that complements Universal Analytics by showing you every action individual users take on your site.

2. Conducting Audience Surveys

User surveys should never be utilized for research on new features or services because people are not very good at predicting whether or not they will buy something in the future. They are, however, ideal for discovering two types of information: demographics and intent.

1. **Demographics:** Do the people who use your site make more or less than a certain amount per year, for example? How many computers are in their household? Because the questions are asking for facts rather than opinions or experiences, these surveys can be delivered to your mailing list.
2. **Intent:** What do your visitors want to do or learn when they come to your site? Was it easy for them to use? Did they find what they needed? Services like iPerceptions. com and Fluidsurveys.com ask these questions when your visitors are actually on the site, which means you get your visitors reactions in the moment.

Audience surveys should be as short as possible. Ask only what you need to know, because the longer the survey, the more likely it is people will exit before finishing. Avoid asking questions you can answer with your own data, such as household income if you already have verifiable data on average household income for your site visitors. Your audience is doing you a favor by taking your survey, so you only want to spend that goodwill for useful and actionable data that you can't get any other way.

One important thing to note: quantitative analysis requires *quantity*. Quantitative user polling requires a representative sample so that you can safely assume that the insights you glean from trends in the data will apply to the majority of your users. Services like SurveyMonkey and Google Website Survey include analytics tools that can tell you if you've gotten enough survey respondents to produce statistically significant results. These services, and others like them, also provide assistance with writing effective survey questions.

Once you have collected quantitative and/or qualitative data, you can use it to create a set of user personas and empathy maps, tools that are the backbone of a strong content strategy.

Putting Audience Research To Work

Once you've conducted enough audience research, distill the collected information down to inform content approaches. Two common and useful tools for doing this are user personas and empathy maps.

User Personas

A user persona is a research-based fictional character who represents the attributes, needs, wants, and behaviors of a group of customers. Converting your quantitative and qualitative research into a set of user personas is a technique to improve the customer-centricity of a product or service by developing a fact-based understanding of your users. User personas will help you decide which content to keep, expand or throw away.

User personas often contain the following material:

- Basics: Name, Gender, Age, Job Title, Household Income, Geographic Information.
- Attributes and Behaviors: What are this user persona's relevant characteristics?
- Attitudes and Beliefs: How does this user persona think and feel about relevant issues?
- Challenges: What are the three relevant problems this user persona needs to solve?
- Solutions: How does your product solve those problems?
- Influencers: Who is most influential in helping this user persona make a decision? This can include publications, TV shows, celebrities, and friends.
- Language: What words, phrases and topics resonate with this user persona?
- Channels: What channels do they use to get information, entertainment? What social media channels do they participate in?

It's tempting to answer these questions based on what seems right instead of actual research, but resist! A user persona based on a mental image of your customer can lead targeting efforts wildly astray. Personas are only as useful as the data you gather to validate them. Instead, create personas based on *actual* data produced from existing customers and metrics produced from web analytics and social networks.

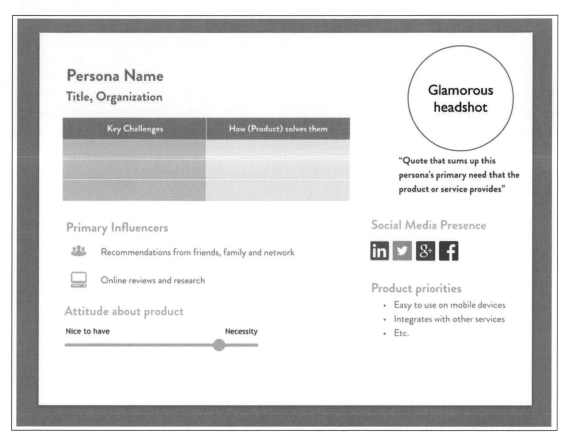

Figure 2.7 Well researched user personas can help you make decisions about the kind of content most likely to capture your target audience's interests. For a printable user persona template, visit the *Return on Engagement* website at www.returnonengagement.net

Empathy Maps

Empathy mapping is a technique to help you visualize what your customers are thinking, hearing, seeing, and doing when they interact with your content in a specific location. No one uses a product or service in a vacuum, so it's important to think through potential distractions and challenges in the context of use.

Another benefit of creating an empathy map is that it allows designers and developers to work together to consider the perspectives of many different types of customers at the same time. It's an alternative to the more time-intensive process of creating a series of narrowly focused user personas or characters that represent the perspective of a single hypothetical website visitor (e.g., a male college graduate, age 42).

By working with empathy maps to identify an audience's high level needs and wishes, you can quickly and efficiently uncover opportunities to enhance user experience.

You can create an empathy map in three easy steps:

1. Draw or place a picture of a typical or actual customer at the center of the map.
2. Create areas around the customer photo that organizes what the customer hears, sees, thinks, and does.
3. Add details to the appropriate branches. Consider using post-it notes or a dry erase board to move details from one section to another as needed.

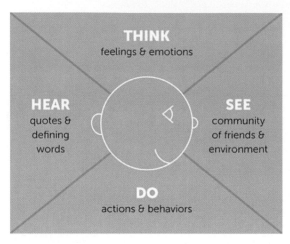

Figure 2.8 Empathy maps help you think through the context in which your target audience is experiencing your content. For a printable empathy map, visit the *Return on Engagement* website at www.returnonengagement.net

Content Planning

Now that you've done research on who your customers are, what channels they use, and what words and phrases they use to describe their pain points, you can begin to create a plan for content. The tools and tactics covered in this section are used by content strategists to develop their work—they are the meat and potatoes of content strategy. Each one helps keep you focused on the twin goals of content strategy: meeting audience needs and meeting business goals.

Message Architecture

A solid content plan begins with message architecture. Message architecture establishes concrete, shared terminology that guides content development across teams and channels. It is what brings together your organizational messaging (business goals) with terms and keywords that meet your customers' needs (audience goals), and should be developed based on your user personas and keywords. Each audience and business goal should have at least one key message attached. Ideally, any team member should be able to clearly understand message architecture and create content that aligns with mutually understood goals. For an editable message architecture worksheet, visit the *Return on Engagement* website at www.returnonengagement.net.

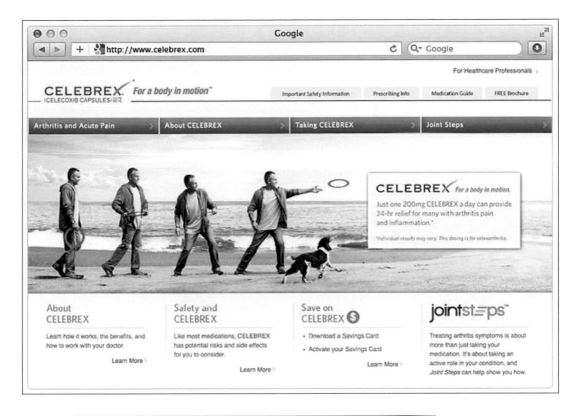

Brand Promise:	Celebrex provides 24-hour relief from arthritis pain.

Audience Needs	Key Messages
1. I feel limited by my condition	1. I have freedom to go do the things I love
	2. I can move my body with a free range of motion
2. Distrust of branded information	3. (Imagery is framed around a person's experience)

Business Attributes	Key Messages
1. Drug information	1. Learn how it works
2. Safety	2. Potential risks
3. Cost	3. Save on Celebrex

Figure 2.9 This is a simple message architecture for an arthritis medication, Celebrex.

Identifying Channels

Content planning also starts with identifying which channels you'll use to publish content. Channels are any communication platforms relevant to your audience and goals. This could include billboards, magazines, brochures, direct mail, sell sheets, videos, and so on. Digital-specific channels include websites, apps, online videos, emails, games, social media, and so on.

Your goal is to figure out which channels your audience most often uses and to adapt your stories for that channel format. Don't waste time creating content for channels your customers don't use, or don't use very often.

Your quantitative and qualitative research should help you identify the best channels as long as it addresses how your audience accesses content. Are they at home at their desk or in the store searching on their phone? Are they browsing, or do they need to find information fast? Which social networks do they frequent?

As always, you must also consider your business goals in addition to the user's needs. To identify the channels favored by your audience that make most sense for you, start with these questions:

- Are we already using the channels our users frequent?
- What actions do you want users to take when accessing content? Are those actions possible using this channel?
- Is user-generated content an option, given time and budget constraints? (This may require significant governance resources.)
- How will you track results on this channel?
- Is this channel cost-effective?
- Do we have the staff resources to create and maintain content on this channel?

Editorial Calendars

Once you've established your channels, you can begin to develop an editorial calendar—the backbone of your content plan. Here you'll organize the major pieces of content you plan to produce and when they'll be published. How you create and maintain an editorial calendar will depend on the size of your team and the resources you have to accomplish ongoing content creation and execution. Project management tools like Basecamp or even a simple calendar application can help greatly with this process. There are also content strategy-specific online tools—like Compendium.com, for example—that offer a more robust platform for managing a calendar.

Think About "The Internet of Things"

"The Internet of Things," a term proposed in 1999 by MIT technologist Kevin Ashton, moves beyond mobile phones and tablets to consider ubiquitous devices like smart refrigerators, thermostats, cars, and any other platform where content might be experienced. Though not applicable to all content, it is increasingly possible that your content could end up on many platforms where the concept of a 'browser' doesn't necessarily apply. Thus, along with considering users, content strategists should:

- Consider devices and how they are used
- Consider the role of different platforms in experiencing content
- Consider web standards whenever possible

Assigning blog topics to team members and ensuring you cover relevant industry events or seasonal topics is much easier when tasks are outlined in a spreadsheet and assigned due dates. Be sure to set realistic expectations with your team (and yourself). If you expect co-workers to write one blog post per month, for instance, make sure they clearly understand what is needed and provide them with the time, editorial support, and schedule to help them succeed. For an editable editorial calendar, visit the *Return on Engagement* website at www.returnonengagement.net.

	Holidays, events	Content description	Content type	Content category	Series category	Author	Design assets needed	Editor
Dec 1-7								
Monday 2	Cyber Monday	Holiday giving	Blog post	Our company		Katherine	Screenshots	Sarah
Tuesday 3								
Wednesday 4		Holiday giving email	Email newsletter				- Template design (Amber) - Images (Amber)	
Thursday 5		Alternatives to a web carousel	Blog post	Design		Buddy	Screenshots (Buddy)	
Friday 6		Kevin Ma's internship re-cap	Blog post	Our company		Kevin Ma		Katherine

Figure 2.10 An inside look at a Mightybytes Editorial Calendar.

Channel and Velocity Plans

Channel and velocity plans work in conjunction with your editorial calendar to establish a publishing schedule for all your content. Your editorial calendar outlines what content you'll create and who will create it, while channel and velocity plans help plan your content distribution for the web, mapping out which outlets you'll publish to and with what frequency.

Channel Plan

Your channel plan outlines the outlets you will use to distribute content, which you identified with the help of your audience research. This includes your website, email marketing, and social media channels. A thorough channel plan will also include notes on message structure, target audience and desired action for each channel. This will help you identify the right types of content to share on each channel and what your calls to action (if any) will be.

You can also include your intended frequency in a channel plan. This is known as velocity. For an editable channel planning document, visit the *Return on Engagement* website at www.returnonengagement.net.

Channel	Velocity	Structure	Desired Action
Mobile site			
Email	Once a week for 6 weeks	75–100 word message, pictures if applicable and a conversion link	Click through to the site and register for a savings card.
Website			
Newsletters			

Figure 2.11 Adapt this Channel Plan template to include all your digital channels.

Velocity Plan

A velocity plan is an outline of the frequency with which you will publish certain types of content on the web. Your velocity plan can be as simple as noting how often you'll publish to your established channels, or it can include long-term content details that map to campaigns and themes. For example, if you create content devoted to holistic wellness, sharing cold remedies every winter might not be a bad idea. If you're doing a ticket giveaway in advance of an event, the number of times you tweet each day might increase as the event date grows nearer.

Velocity plans are also great tools for reusing content. Popular seasonal topics can be re-shared on an annual basis, as long as the content remains relevant. Repetition strengthens impressions and relationships.

You should be particularly mindful that while publishing frequently helps your search engine rankings and sharing frequently on social channels boosts your site traffic, to maximize returns on social networks you must be helpful and useful. If your content is repetitive, irrelevant, or impersonal, it will fall flat and your efforts will be wasted.

There are lots of different velocity models for different channels and types of content. Here are a few examples, and for an editable velocity planning document, visit the *Return on Engagement* website at www.returnonengagement.net.

Channel: Twitter

Subject: Event

Velocity:

• Execute a ticket giveaway three weeks in advance of an event.

• Promote different aspects of the event every third day for three weeks.

• Rotate between different target time slots within a target time zone:

    - 9–10 am for press announcements

    - Prime time television for consumers

January	February	March	April	May	June
Healthy recipes for your resolutions	Baking with fruits and veggies	First spring vegetables recipes	Using up your Easter eggs	Labor day grilling	Strawberry and melon recipes

• Monthly velocity plan mapped to flu season.

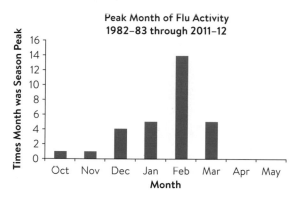

Newsletter messages by month	
October	Schedule your flu shot
November	Flu shot efficacy
December	Healthy holiday travel tips
January	There's still time to get a flu shot
February	How to take care of flu patients
March	Aren't you glad you got your flu shot?

Figure 2.12 These are velocity plans for a Twitter feed, blog series, and monthly newsletter.

Content Specification Document

A content specification document is a set of rules for each channel and type of content that both copywriters and developers can use as a blueprint to guide their work. You should work toward the goal of arming a copywriter with the tools necessary to match specifications for each piece of content. Likewise, if you share this document with UX designers, they should have ample resources to create site wireframes and page layouts. For each content type, define message, audience, and conversion goals. As you can see in this example, specific instructions for each individual content type—in this case a teaser—are included.

When you've sketched out guidelines for all content types, you end up with a blueprint that includes:

- A format for every heading, subheading, and paragraph with word counts
- Notes on what pages the content should link to
- Notes on photography and other multimedia content that includes specific brand attributes
- Storyboards for videos, if applicable
- Whether content exists for this page already or not
- Who is responsible for it

> **Sample format for Teaser copy**
>
> **Headline: 2-3 words including keyword**
> Example: Transforming [fill in the blank: Mobile Banking, Health, Retail Customer Experiences, City Government, Telecommunications, etc.]
>
> **Teaser copy:**
> 10-25 words (1-2 sentences), describing how BOA is transforming a specific vertical or introducing a benefits proposition.
> Include related keywords in description.
>
> **Call to action:**
> 2-3 words, inviting user to explore the related page.
>
> **Photography:**
> Photographs help your user find the landing page that relates most to them and visually confirm that BOA works with clients like them.

Figure 2.13 Content specification documents also make it easy for anyone to jump in and write a piece of content that's aligned with your strategy.

While creating this document takes a bit of time on the front end, it simplifies the process for writers, developers, and designers creating new content, because they'll have a blueprint to work from. For a sample content specfication planning document, visit the *Return on Engagement* website at www.returnonengagement.net.

Content Audits

Use a content audit to assess the existing content on your site. Content audits identify both gaps to be filled and content to be revised or redirected. Leaving outdated or irrelevant content on your site detracts from your quality content and may confuse and ultimately turn off visitors.

Auditing every single site page will offer the most thorough understanding of all outdated content. But if that's not an option due to time or resource constraints, consider auditing a sample of the site, such as the main landing pages, most visited subsections, or your most popular blog category. This should give you a good sense of what needs to be added, edited, or updated without drowning you in excess work.

Content audits are ideal for:

- Scoping and revising an existing website with extensive content.
- Managing political issues around departmental ownership of content.
- Assessing existing print and digital content resources for potential repurposing.

Your content audit will record quantitative information that will help you answer qualitative questions about how your content is performing.

Quantitative Information: Objective Details

- How is it organized? What are the main sections and sub pages?
- What content do you have AND how much of it do you have? That's not just copy, it's everything: video, PDFs, registrations forms, etc.

- Is everything up to date and in compliance with company or legal standards?
- Who created it (which department)?
- How much traffic has this page generated? What is the bounce rate? What are your traffic sources?
- How much traffic came from social media?
- What other pages does this site link to?
- Who owns final approval? This comes into play when you've got really complex sites that represent more than one department, company, or brand.

Qualitative: Is the Content Any Good?

- Is it still relevant to your users and your business goals?
- Is it right for the channel?
- Is it useful to users?

Here is a template for a simple content audit. For an editable content audit document, visit the *Return on Engagement* website at www.returnonengagement.net.

Figure 2.14 The structure is simple, but don't let that fool you—content audits are a ton of work!

Social Media Optimization

Social Media Optimization (often called SMO) can drive qualified traffic to your site using social networks. "Optimizing" for social media simply means you're making it easy for your audience to share your content via their social networks. You can do this by including social sharing buttons on your content, such as blog posts, but you can also optimize for social media by sharing content on the right channels at the right time. For instance, if a California-based surfboard company has an active Twitter following in Australia, they'll likely need to schedule some content at times the Australian audience is actually awake. You should take SMO into account when building your channel and velocity plans.

Adapting Content

How do you create enough content to publish across all these channels? Your existing content can be revised, tweaked and reformatted for different channels. For example, a blog post could be broken into a series of tweets. Key points in a video could be repurposed for a white paper. An infographic, hosted on your site, might perform well on Pinterest. A blog series might make for a popular webinar.

Maintaining a working spreadsheet of all your content can help you map existing content to new channels.

Content Governance

In small organizations, content rules are often informal. When people have a close relationship to a business or work on small teams, content that serves the dual needs of audience and business can happen naturally, without written rules. But as an organization grows more complex, it may become necessary to formalize the management of content strategy. This is known as content governance.

A governance model—even if it is unwritten—is an *understanding* of who creates content and who manages social media. In large organizations with complex content needs, a written content governance model provides structure to establish ownership, define approval processes, and continuously evaluate content and technical resources to ensure that all content is meeting the dual needs of the organization and its audience. Think of your governance model as a business plan for your content strategy. It's a living document that defines how your organization currently operates and includes plans for contingency and growth.

Like a content audit, there is no single format for a content governance model, but a basic model might include:

- Who is responsible for creating and maintaining content
- What written documents exist that outline how content is created and maintained
- What business standards are we responsible for upholding
- What audience needs must we address
- Technical limitations and capabilities
- Budgets
- Review processes

Content Resource Assessment:
- Who is responsible for creating each piece of content?
- What is the content's lifecycle?
- What business goal does it serve?

Tech Resource Assessment:
- What content can be realistically supported by the site?
- Who tags content?

Quality Assurance:
- What is the review process?
- Who owns the final approval?

Channel and Velocity:
- How often will the content be updated?
- How often are messages repeated?
- What channels will the content be delivered through?

Figure 2.15 Establishing a governance plan helps keep your content creation train on the track.

- Staff structure
- Contingency plans—how will we handle crisis?

For an editable content governance document, visit the *Return on Engagement* website at www.returnonengagement.net.

Conclusion

Effective content strategy helps you tie content-driven marketing goals to customer needs while improving search engine rankings in the process, which results in more qualified customer traffic to your website. Your potential customers are online for a reason. What are they looking for? What channels are they searching? What devices are they using? Your goal is to figure out the answers to these questions so that you can develop content that is valuable to your audiences and deliver it where and when they need it.

The concepts we covered in this chapter include:

- Using your organization's unique story and assets to create content so seductive that your audiences won't be able to resist reading, using, and sharing it.
- An overview of content strategy artifacts, including content specification documents, content audits, message architecture, and a range of other tools. For editable content strategy templates and worksheets, visit the *Return on Engagement* website at www.returnonengagement.net.
- Basic strategies for optimizing your content for different social media platforms.
- Manage content creation across your organization with governance and maintenance plans.

Profile

Sarah Best
Content and Social Media Director, Mightybytes
Mightybytes' Content and Social Media Director, Sarah Best, shares her thoughts below on the challenge of scaling social media programs, governance, and more.

Sarah is an award-winning content and social media strategist. As one of Foursquare's first business partners, Sarah wrote and launched four Foursquare badges, growing her client's business page from 0 followers to over 120,000. As a content strategist, Sarah helps a range of clients get to know their customers and develop the content that best suits both business and customer objectives. Sarah's past clients and partners include Rails

Figure 2.16 Sarah Best, Content and Social Media Director, Mightybytes

to Trails Conservancy, Michelin, the Apple Store, the Art Institute of Chicago, the City of Chicago and more. Her awards include Best Use of Social Media Platform (Travel + Leisure Magazine, 2012), and others for social media marketing (Communicator Awards, North American Travel Journalists). She was named the #1 North American Influencer for Social Media Week (Synthesio, 2011). She also fostered community as a Meet Up host at SXSW Interactive 2014.

What is content strategy?

Content strategy is a term that is used to describe a field that has emerged in the past five years or so. Content strategy acknowledges that the terminology and approaches used to manage print publications around a monthly editorial calendar are no longer adequate to manage the complex world that we live in, which has multitudinous content channels that all have their own rules of engagement, their own tone and audiences, and which operate at different velocities.

The web is a living thing that expands and contracts, and its audiences are diverse and move from platform to platform like schools of fish, never fully unifying or dissipating but sometimes coalescing around certain cultural moments and ideas. Content channels are the reefs that help facilitate this behavior.

Content strategy is a set of tools and tactics that deals with this complexity, just as in mathematics, chaos theory sets out to explain the behavior of dynamic systems that are hard to predict, like the weather.

Where do the disciplines of content strategy and user experience design overlap?

To me, content strategy and user experience design are two sides of the same coin. My own content strategy practice is rooted in user research and empathy. What are their needs and desires? What challenges do they face? And how do we balance those needs with business objectives? Additionally, what devices are they using in what contexts? How do you make the customer's experience both useful and compelling? I think those are questions that both content strategists and user experience designers ask.

Where content strategy diverges from user experience is with a concern with how to engage users across a number of different channels, such as through social media platforms, a drip marketing campaign executed via email, and different parts of a website. Velocity also comes into play in content strategy—understanding the rhythm of Twitter, versus the rhythm of Facebook, and so on.

Content, web, email, social, search: How do you see it all fitting together?

They're all channels through which you can reach audiences, and you should consider which are most important to meeting your audience's and your business's objectives.

What can the field of marketing and the field of communications learn from each other?

I think that marketing often starts with a concern with conversions: how many people am I converting to a sale, and at what cost? Because traditional communications is based in the idea of earning unpaid media placements, I think there is more of an emphasis placed on the value of strategic partnerships: what companies and organizations can I partner with to extend the audience of my brand? Also on relationship building: what influencers have extended the reach of my content this week?

There is a lot to value in both approaches. Learning how to tie social media efforts to a dollar amount can be extremely valuable in communicating a return on investment to business stakeholders, but so can strategically thinking about partnerships as a vehicle for attracting new audiences and generating media placements.

What is the key to a successful strategic partnership?

The key to successful partnerships is to start a conversation with a potential partner with an open mind and open language: How can we work together do something that is mutually beneficial? That is how I made the partnership with Foursquare happen. By pitching my team as having the relationships with press, influencers, and consumers in a market that they didn't yet have a foothold in, Chicago. And that successful partnership opened the door to many others, including promotional partnerships with local media, Southwest Airlines, local restaurants, theaters and cultural institutions.

How has your career changed since the first edition of *Return on Engagement*? What do you do differently on a daily basis than you did several years ago?

I used to spend my days communicating with tens of thousands of followers through social media, and to millions of customers through a branded website. There are some patterns of engagement that are easier to see and understand if you are working with a huge group of people. I came into that position at a time when social media tactics were not particularly well defined, and I had the freedom to experiment across a lot of platforms, every day, on a massive scale, to see what worked and didn't work.

Today, I spend less time on the ground, and more time applying what I've learned to the content and social media strategies of clients in diverse sectors. My clients come to me not quite knowing who their online audiences are; not knowing what content to develop for a new website or what to do about all their old content; or not having a strategy for what to do after the launch of their site. Helping customers develop a more sophisticated understanding of what their customers are doing online, and how to better communicate their brand through strategic messages, is very rewarding.

What has been the biggest change in the world of social media marketing over the past few years?

Scalability is always a challenge. In an ideal world, we could use platforms like Twitter to listen to every individual customer's needs and to meet those needs quickly and efficiently. In the real world, there is never enough time to do a perfect job of this. That is why I spend time helping clients prioritize key messages and to discover what channels are most effective for reaching their target audiences. We have to think strategically, because there is only so much time in the day.

Conversely, I find that the biggest challenge that most of my clients face, is producing content within a certain business environment. Almost everyone at some point comes to me with questions about governance: how do they get a particular department or stakeholder's buy in? How do they solve the problem of having too many departments want too many things on a homepage? How do they do the work that they need to do while facing certain staffing constraints? That is what governance tools such as workflows, approval and review processes, and written policies solve.

What will be the biggest challenge for marketing firms wanting to stay relevant moving forward?

While it's always a challenge to keep up with what the latest Instagram or Pinterest is, at your core you just have to have a practice that is based in something deeper than that, whether it's based in usability or in something else. The fish will swim from reef to reef, but we can observe some patterns in their behaviors that translate from one platform to another.

Similarly, what will be the biggest challenge for web design firms wanting to stay relevant moving forward?

I think the biggest challenge is keeping up with audience contexts. According to Amit Singhal, a Senior Vice President of Google, the ideal future technology is one that fades into the background when you don't need it. Physical devices such as mobile phones can present barriers to the user that separate them in unnatural ways from the world around them. With gestural interfaces, native language search, geolocation and devices like Google Glass, those barriers keep breaking down.

Mobile phones have already exploded the idea of user experience to encompass dynamic and unstable scenarios, such as people who are tweeting about a natural disaster in real time, or to give a more mundane example, people who are price-checking something at an electronics store to make sure that they are getting the best deal.

Those dynamic situations are just going to keep getting more and more complex, with more and more design patterns and audience contexts to consider.

What is the difference between content marketing and influencer engagement?

I always try to identify situations that are mutually beneficial to both the customer and the business. I think that "content marketing" can sometimes be too narrowly focused on conversions at the expense of meeting a customer's needs and desires.

Good influencer engagement can produce a return on engagement while facilitating a relationship rather than just a conversion. You still get the conversions, but you also foster customer loyalty.

An example of this from my own career was when I started a program in Chicago for amateur photographers, who had the need to develop their skills and a desire to explore new parts of the city. They also interacted with other photographers online through Flickr (and subsequently through Instagram) but hadn't yet met each other in real life. My client had a need to source authentic photography of Chicago without paying a lot of money for it.

The win-win situation that I came up with was to host events for photographers where they could develop their photography skills with local teachers, gain more knowledge about Chicago's neighborhoods through guided tours, and meet their online friends for the first time in real life, over drinks. I provided them with teachers, space to gather in, and thoughtfully facilitated events. This cost almost nothing beyond paying the teachers, since my office already had space and knowledgeable guides at our disposal, as well as relationships with restaurants and bars who were willing to donate drinks and appetizers.

The business benefit was that we ended up with photography that was higher quality, better annotated, and with relationships with photographers that we could leverage when we needed photo content. It also led to photo walk event partnerships with the Apple Store, Art Institute of Chicago, Hancock Observatory and other businesses and organizations.

The benefit to the photographers was equally clear: they were gaining new skills and engaging in peer-to-peer education, exploring unique locations around the city they might not normally have access to, and forming lasting friendships with other photographers. The meet ups that I organized resulted in an independent group of over 400 photographers who still organize photo walks around different areas of Chicago on their own. I myself met some of my best friends in the group.

Where do you see the industry evolving?

On the technical side, continuing development of gestural interfaces and natural language based search is fundamentally changing user experience design. On the marketing and communications side, what I am seeing is people innovating strategies using existing platforms to solve more and more complex problems, such as preventing violence and communicating effectively during natural disasters and political uprising.

Anything else you want to share?

I think it's crucial to remember that people in different cultures and situations use the internet in radically different ways. Read case studies about people making billions of dollars in financial microtransactions through m-pesas (mobile banking) in Africa. Think about grandparents accessing the internet through a proxy like a grandchild ("Could you look this up for me?"). Think about how people with limited mobility or vision use the internet. Think about how toddlers use tablets. I love to study edge cases and to read case studies outside of my discipline, because it expands my sense of the strategies and tools that are available to me, even in less extreme circumstances.

Note

1. This information has been rewritten from content available at The Moz Blog, April 10, 2013, "How to Build a Content Marketing Strategy," www.seomoz.org/blog/how-to-build-a-content-marketing-strategy.

CHAPTER THREE

SEO and Content Strategy

Search Engine Optimization (SEO) is an online marketing strategy for driving qualified search engine traffic by increasing a page's rank in organic (i.e., unpaid) search engine listings.

A successful SEO strategy is built on a foundation of high quality content. Once the content is in place, you optimize that content for search engines in three ways:

- Identifying and using keywords and search phrases.
- Developing and executing a smart link building strategy.
- Optimizing page metadata.

Identifying and Using Keywords and Search Phrases

People use search engines to find specific information. The words they enter into the search bar represent the primary information the search engine has about the searcher's intent, so search engine algorithms look for content that uses those words. As a content strategist, your goal is to figure out exactly what words your target audience uses to search for the content your organization has created. These words are your keywords, and you'll use them throughout all your content to focus search engine attention on your content.

Broad Term and Long Tail

When people search, they tend to use two types of keywords: broad term and long tail. Broad term words describe your offering in the most general way possible. Long tail words describe your offering in a more specific way. According to the team at Moz, 70% of searches lie[1] in the long tail, hundreds of millions of unique searches that are done just a few times per day.

For example, a realtor might use this set of broad term and long tail keywords:

Broad Term	Long Tail
Realtor	Ranch-style homes for sale
Home for sale	Homes for sale by owner in Chicago
New home(s) for sale	Best Chicago real estate agents

Principles for Choosing Keywords

Your keywords can and should change over time based on performance data, so choose keywords with the mindset that you're testing hypotheses rather than laying down permanent rules. The rules of thumb we use when we're creating keyword lists are:

1. Stick to keyword lists of about 20 or so terms and phrases.
2. Use a mix of broad term and long tail terms. There is a lot of competition for broad terms—think about how many companies want to be the first search result for "wedding planning"—so it's hard to fight to the top of the search rankings using broad terms alone. Ranking at the top for a long tail term like "DIY photo booth" is a much more attainable goal.
3. Include 2–4 word phrases. This is partly because it's how people search and partly because phrases are less competitive and more targeted to what you offer.
4. Always do a relevance check on your keywords. Terms that seem like a good fit for your content may prove to have associations that are less relevant to your organization. For example, a realtor might consider using the term "affordable housing." However, a quick Google search of "affordable housing" shows that the top results are all for government assistance. For a realtor, "cheap apartments" conveys the same idea without the government associations.

Keyword Tools

There are a bunch of tools you can use to identify the best keywords for your content strategy. Here are several:

Free Options (most require an account)

- **Google Keyword Planner** (adwords.google.com/keywordplanner) is a replacement for the erstwhile Google Keyword Tool that now uses functionality from that and their Traffic Estimator tool. A Google AdWords account is required.
- **Wordtracker** (freekeywords.wordtracker.com) gives you free access to their keyword tool (with an account), but they also have a paid suite of online marketing tools as well.
- **SEOBook's Keyword Tool** (tools.seobook.com/keyword-tools/seobook/) is free, but like Wordtracker also offers premium options.

Paid Options

All three of these options offer a suite of tools with a paid subscription, one of which is a keyword tool.

- Moz (moz.com/tools/keyword-difficulty)
- SEMrush (semrush.com)
- Hubspot (www.hubspot.com/products/seo)

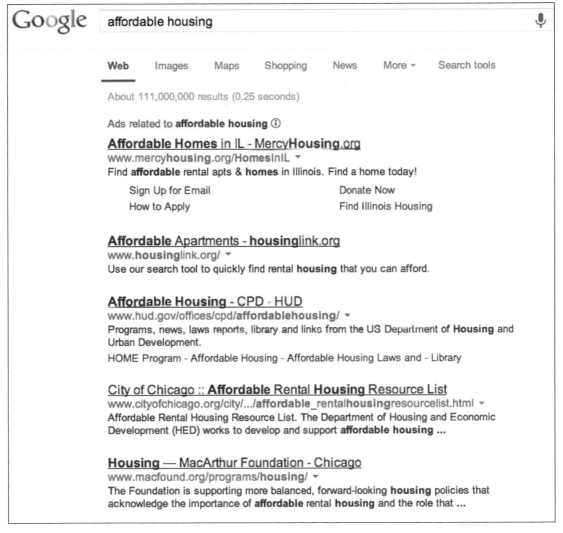

Figure 3.1 Always do a relevance check on your keywords to ensure that you are using terms with the right connotation (see also 3.2).

Link Building

Search engines see links from reputable websites as votes representing internet user's choices about what pages are relevant and important. Link building is an SEO technique aimed at increasing the number and quality of sites that link to your page. While none of the search engines publish guidelines outlining exactly how they measure link building, there are a handful of principles content strategists can usefully plan around:

Google PageRank

Google's PageRank algorithm assesses the trustworthiness of the sites that link to you and assigns your site a number from 0 to 10. For years content strategists used their site's PageRank number as the Key Performance Indicator for their work.

Then in October 2009, Google employee Susan Moskwa noted, "We've been telling people for a long time that they shouldn't focus on PageRank so much; many site owners seem to think it's the most important metric for them to track, which is simply not true."[2]

Your site's PageRank should merely be considered a helpful indication of its authority as opposed to the 'be-all-end-all' metric to focus on. Instead, focus on metrics that will help the relevancy of your site in business terms, like conversion rates.

Create Link-worthy Site Content

This is the ultimate trick to building links. It's also Google's own top recommendation for ranking. It works like this:

- **Create** a truly great piece of content. Original research, detailed how-to content and useful tools are especially effective for this approach.
- **Align** the post or page with a keyphrase. Find a phrase that people are searching for and a phrase that isn't too competitive. Use basic on-page SEO when writing the page to make sure it's indicating its relevance for the phrase.
- **Post and share** it with a few bloggers who are interested in the topic. Again, social media is useful for this. Personal emails can also be effective. Bring the content to their attention and politely suggest they cover the topic on their blogs, if it isn't too awkward.

Most content strategists are focused on creating link-worthy content for their own organization's website (or the client for whom they are doing strategy). Guest blogging, however, is often overlooked because the content is offsite. Still, if content you create for other sites links back to your website (in your bio, for instance), it adds value in the form of inbound links. Thus guest blogging should be considered an important part of your channel plans or other strategic content initiatives.

Metadata

Metadata is data about data. People can understand information if presented in text, images, charts, videos, and so on, but search algorithms can only read text. In order to ensure that the content presented in images and videos can be included in search engine rankings, we label those files with machine readable text tags. These tags are metadata.

Your page title tags, image alt tags, link anchor text, and even file names should adhere to your keyword strategy just like on-page content should. This practice will ensure that your site's content is being indexed correctly by search engines.

Which tags are most relevant to the "crawlability" of your website by search engines? Here are some commonly used metadata tags relevant to how a search engine interprets a web page.

Meta Description

This tag provides search engines with a short description about the content on the page. When your page appears on a search result list, your meta description is the snippet of information the person searching sees. Although algorithms no longer rely heavily on meta description, people still do. According to a survey conducted by iAcquire and SurveyMonkey, 43% of people click on a result because the meta description best matches what they're looking for.[3] The length limit for meta description is just 155 characters, so all your practice composing witty Tweets will pay off here. It is also important to note that this description is what typically shows up when you share links via social networks like Facebook or LinkedIn.

Sustainable Web Design: A Blog Series | Mightybytes
www.mightybytes.com/blog/entry/**sustainable-web-design**/ ▾
by Tim Frick - in 352 Google+ circles
Jan 4, 2013 - Mightybytes announces a new blog series about **sustainable web design**, which will help you create a greener, cleaner web.

Figure 3.3 The text in the red box is the meta description of this page.

Page Title

The title tag defines the name of an HTML document. The title shows up in two places: in the top of the web browser and in a search engine results page (SERP). Because the title tag has a big influence on search engine rankings, it's an important place to lead with keywords (but make sure it sounds natural, as it is one of the few tags visible to humans). You're limited to a mere 70 characters. It is best to place your keywords in the beginning when possible.

Mightybytes – Web Design, Illinois B Corp | Design-Driven Media

◄ ► ⬆ 🔲 http://www.mightybytes.com/   ↻ Reader ⬇

```
<meta http-equiv="Content-Type" content="text/html" charset="UTF-8" />

<title>Mightybytes - Web Design, Illinois B Corp | Design-Driven Media</title>

<link rel="profile" href="http://gmpg.org/xfn/11" />
<link rel="pingback" href="http://www.mightybytes.com/xmlrpc.php" />
```

Figure 3.4 The text in the red box is the Page Title.

Heading Tags

Search engines look to heading tags to gauge the relevance of a page's content. The H1 tag is the most important because it identifies the content of the page. Each page only gets one H1 tag, so treat them the way newspapers treat headlines: attention grabbing and full of keywords. Heading tags range in six sizes—h1, h2, h3, h4, h5 and h6 (naturally). As they denote a web page's information hierarchy, these tags should only be used at the appropriate places; it's the rare web page with enough content to justify six separate sub-heading levels!

Figure 3.5 The title of this blog post (in the red box) is the H1 tag. This image also includes the H1 tag information in the CSS.

Rel = Author and Rel = Publisher Tags

Google is increasingly giving Google+ more relevance to search engines. One manifestation of this is that Google will begin ranking content connected to authors they deem credible over content that is not. And, you guessed it: Google uses the author information in Google+ accounts to identify credible authors. That's reason enough in and of itself to get a G+ account if you don't already have one.

Alt Tag Optimization

Alt tags provide relevant descriptive information for site crawlers of image, video, and graphic file assets on web pages. Proper use of this metadata means your content can

Figure 3.6 The text in the red box is the alt tag. This image also shows what the alt tag looks like in the CSS.

more easily be ranked in image searches. Alt tags should accurately describe the image. For example, "chart" is not as good an alt tag as "American population growth chart."

Other Metadata Considerations

Though the above tags are the most popular in terms of search engine crawls, here are some other important considerations for getting a website indexed properly. These may be less directly related to content strategy than some of the above options, but they are important nonetheless.

Robots.txt File

A robots.txt file is a simple text file at the root of your website's server directory that is used to prohibit search engine bots from crawling a particular page or set of pages. You define which pages the site crawler should ignore. This file must be named as robots.txt in order to work.

Website Navigation

A website that is easy to navigate will help visitors find information they are looking for. Well-organized site navigation also helps search engines index and categorize pages. HTML and XML site maps, in tandem with web services like Google Webmaster Tools, ensure that search engines will understand how your website is structured.

Similarly, internal hypertext linking between pages on your site will help search engines better understand how pages relate to each other content-wise. This is an important consideration for content strategists, as these links should use keyword-rich anchor text.

Anchor Text

Also known as link label or link title, the anchor text of a hyperlink is what a user actually reads in the links on your site. Clearly written, keyword-rich anchor text will help users understand where links lead, and also help search engines interpret what a page is all about based on other pages that link to it and where it links to.

Avoid the following when creating hypertext links:

- Using general anchor texts, like "click here."
- Using anchor text that is not related to the content of the web page it sits on.
- Using long sentences.
- Creating unnecessary links.

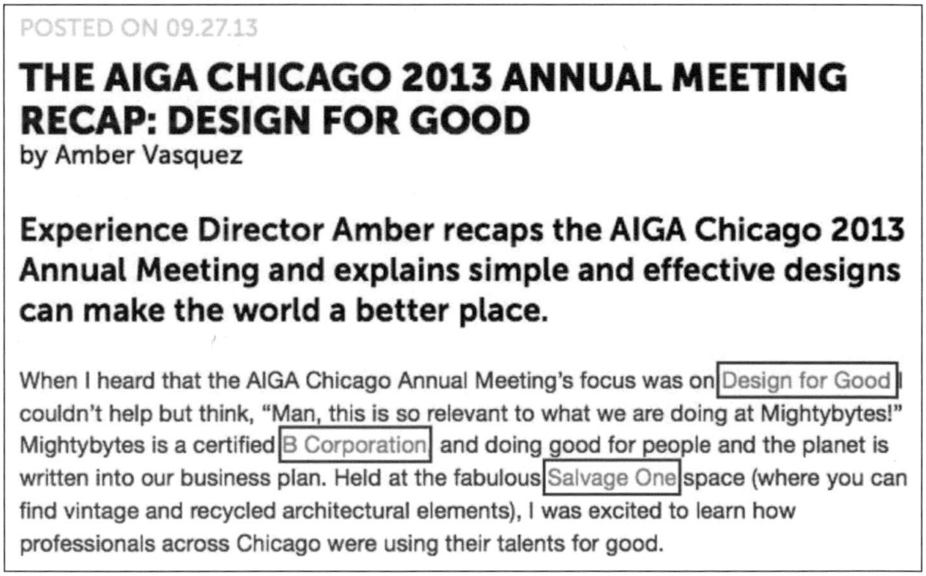

POSTED ON 09.27.13

THE AIGA CHICAGO 2013 ANNUAL MEETING RECAP: DESIGN FOR GOOD
by Amber Vasquez

Experience Director Amber recaps the AIGA Chicago 2013 Annual Meeting and explains simple and effective designs can make the world a better place.

When I heard that the AIGA Chicago Annual Meeting's focus was on Design for Good I couldn't help but think, "Man, this is so relevant to what we are doing at Mightybytes!" Mightybytes is a certified B Corporation and doing good for people and the planet is written into our business plan. Held at the fabulous Salvage One space (where you can find vintage and recycled architectural elements), I was excited to learn how professionals across Chicago were using their talents for good.

Figure 3.7 In this image, all three anchor text links are boxed in red. Note that not a single one says "click here."

URL Structure

A URL that clearly states the page's content makes it easier for search engines to correctly index your site. Creating appropriate filenames and expressive categories on your website will lead to easy to read URLs.

For example, an unfriendly URL structure is www.seotrafficspider.com/seo_articles/15042009.html. Based on that URL, all we know about the content at that address is that it's an article about SEO. SEO is a huge topic, and we have no way of knowing whether or not the content is relevant to our interests. In addition, the category "seo_articles" is vague; it could mean that the content is a list of articles rather than a single article.

A more friendly URL structure is http://moz.com/blog/semantic-SEO-questions. Based on this URL, we know that the content is a blog post about semantic SEO questions. It's much easier for both search engine spiders and people to judge whether or not the content is relevant to their interests.

The Semantic Web

Metadata tags are a stop on the road to the ultimate goal of many engineers: building the semantic web. The semantic web will be structured to enable computers, search engines, mobile devices and any other web-enabled device to interpret all information on the web, from images and videos to interactions between people and computers.

Resource Descriptive Framework-in-attributes and Microformats are two stepping stones to the semantic web.

Resource Descriptive Framework-in-attributes

Resource Description Framework-in-attributes (RDFa) is a tool for embedding rich metadata within web documents. The model enables people to embed RDF triples within XHTML documents and compliant browsers, devices and search engines to extract them.

So what is an RDF triple, you ask? The RDF methodology, in a word, treats attributes like sentence elements, called statements. Large collections of data are broken down into individual statements that are constructed in a particular manner that make them easier to process. Statements typically fall into three categories: subject, predicate, and object, which are used in combination—aptly called a triple—to specify an attribute name/value pair about a particular resource.

- Subject identifies what object the triple is defining.
- Predicate defines the piece of data in the object being given a value.
- Object is the actual value.

The W3C gives a great explanation of why this is important using Albert Einstein as an example. Let's first look at the following statements.

Albert was born on March 14, 1879, in Germany. There is a picture of him at the web address http://en.wikipedia.org/wiki/Image:Albert_Einstein_Head.jpg.

Figure 3.8 Albert is semantic-curious. Aren't you? (Even just a little bit?)

Search engines currently would have some difficulty interpreting this content. If we separate the data into smaller, more manageable statements, it becomes easier to interpret:

- Albert was born on March 14, 1879.
- Albert was born in Germany.
- Albert has a picture at http://en.wikipedia.org/wiki/Image:Albert_Einstein_Head.jpg.

Using the concept of RDFa triples, Albert becomes the subject in all of the above statements. Likewise, the phrases—was born on, has a picture at, and was born in—are the predicates. Finally, the remaining elements—March 14, 1879, Germany and http://en.wikipedia.org/wiki/Image: Albert_Einstein_Head.jpg are the triple's objects.

With the defined structure of RDF in place, this content becomes easier for data applications (i.e., search engines, though the ramifications extend beyond that as well) to interpret.

Easily defining the semantic web very quickly becomes a somewhat esoteric endeavor. Without getting into the details of bnodes, urirefs, and literals, the most important thing to remember is that as more and more web content embraces these standards the nature of what we know as search today will change significantly.

Microformats

In contrast to RDFa, Microformats offer a web-based approach to semantic markup wherein developers can re-use existing XHTML and HTML tags to convey metadata and other attributes. This approach allows information intended for end-users (such as contact information, geographic coordinates, calendar events, etc.) to also be automatically processed by software and search engines.

On the surface, the two systems seem remarkably similar. Both aspire to encode semantic information into web documents so that content can be reused for both humans and machines. In both systems, this goal is achieved by using attributes typically hidden from users to indicate location and contextual meaning of the metadata.

The two systems clash in their methodology, however, resulting in yet another age-old war between computing standards. More people currently use Microformats, but RDFa has been developed by the W3C and uses XML, an existing standard, to provide a scalable format for semantic content. Microformats are supported by a number of browsers as well.

As of this writing, one standard has not emerged supreme over the other, meaning that in addition to creating web content for many different browsers and devices, developers will need to integrate competing data formats as well if they want to support semantic markup in their site pages. Regardless, with its focus on context rather than simple strings of letters and numbers, the semantic web offers the potential to redefine how we find information online.

For a downloadable example of a perfectly meta-data optimized page, visit the *Return on Engagement* website at www.returnonengagement.net.

Conclusion

The ultimate goal of your SEO strategy is to make it easy for your target audience to find the content you've carefully tailored to their interests—not to trick search engine algorithms into ranking your page highly regardless of its relevance to the person searching.

- **Update Frequently.** Regular site content updates trigger search engine crawls. The more your site is crawled by search engines, the more you show up in results.
- **Keep Good Company.** The more high-trust sites that link to you (using keyword-rich anchor text) the higher your page will rank. The higher your page ranks

in results, the more traffic you will get from search engines. If your content is properly targeted using techniques like personas and keyword exercises, the traffic should be qualified as well.

- **Be Social.** Regular social media content updates that add value to members on the network also drive qualified traffic to your site.

Figure 3.9 Co-founder/ Strategic Director, Orbit Media

Profile

Andy Crestodina
Co-founder / Strategic Director, Orbit Media
He's written something like 170 articles on topics like email marketing, search optimization, social media, Analytics and content strategy.

Andy Crestodina is a co-founder of Orbit Media, an award winning, 30-person web design company here in Chicago. Since 2001, Andy has provided web strategy and marketing advice to more than 1000 businesses. He is also the author of Content Chemistry: The Illustrated Handbook for Content Marketing, so he knows his stuff.

What's your strategy for promoting your content?

We're always looking for ways to have a single blog post get traction from all three channels: search, social, and email. In practice, that means every post is promoted in social media. Then every other week, one post becomes the center of the newsletter and is promoted through email as well. These posts are also generally aligned with a keyphrase, so they also rank well in Google.

But it's important to think outside the visit. Social media is about more than content promotion. It's a way to do online network. Email marketing isn't just about driving traffic. It's about keeping in touch with people in the sales funnel. And lastly, making blog posts visible in search isn't just about getting traffic to that post. It's about creating link magnets that support our rank for the more general, lead generating phrases.

What is your publishing schedule?

We do weekly posts on our blog, a weekly guest post on other organization's blogs, bi-weekly email newsletters. In addition, we host monthly events and participate in several big annual programs, including a conference, Content Jam, and an in-kind donation program for non-profits, Chicago Cause.

Is your entire staff involved in publishing content?

It's a challenge for us to get everyone involved. It literally requires a slight shift in our culture. So far about half of us have contributed to the blog, but very few do so regularly. We're working on this.

What are your typical day-to-day marketing tasks and how much time of each day do they take up?

The only real day-to-day activities are social media coverage. But we have a bi-weekly rhythm of writing, editing, publishing, and measurement. I do a lot of writing at night and on weekends. All told, it's two to three hours a day of my time and at least four hours per day from Amanda, our in-house marketer.

Can you explain your process for promoting content?

Sure! Here goes . . .

1. Once you pick your topic, research keywords. We created a best practice on-page SEO checklist for using keywords in our posts, which you can see here: www.orbitmedia. com/blog/seo-best-practices/
2. If it makes sense, get a quote from someone active in social media to add to the article. They'll promote the article to their networks, so it's a nice win-win.
3. Tag the article for Google Authorship and tag anyone you mentioned in the article.
4. Once it's live, write a compelling subject line and send it to your list.
5. Then, share it several time on the social media networks. Your followers may share it with their following.
6. Schedule a few tweets to the post over the next six months.
7. Lastly, if it ranks high on page two or low on page one, look for ways to link to it from other pages, either other posts in your blog or potentially from a new guest post on a popular blog.

How much time do you spend researching keyphrases and targeting SEO techniques to improve content performance?

We are big advocates for keyphrase research because aligning content with phrases and topics is a way to make posts much more visible. I take the extra time to look up phrases and tweak the copy, and as a result we get tons more traffic. I have many posts that are visited 10, 20, or even 50 times per day, just because I found a relevant phrase and did my best to make it the best page on the web for that topic. It's hard work, but it can pay off. There are no real SEO shortcuts.

Notes

1. Moz, "Keyword Research," http://moz.com/beginners-guide-to-seo/keyword-research
2. Susan Moskwa quoted in George Bounacos, "Google PageRank Is Dead—Fast Friday Fact," October 16, 2009, www.sbmteam.com/blog/page-rank
3. "18 Meta Tags Every Webpage Should Have in 2013," February 21, 2013, www.iacquire.com/blog/18-meta-tags-every-webpage-should-have-in-2013/

CHAPTER FOUR

Design Strategy
An Integrated Approach

Designing for digital is about designing for action, not just visual appeal. These actions should help you achieve business and marketing goals, and help your users achieve their goals as well.

Digital design requires synthesizing all the information in your strategic plan to create an engaging and useful experience. Technology, content, interaction design, and navigation should come together on your site to form a seamless user experience that is engaging, easy to understand, and puts any information within as few clicks as possible.

In this chapter, we cover a set of principles for creating an effective design strategy that meets marketing goals. It will include:

- Designing for content
- Designing for technology
- Designing for usability
- Designing for interaction
- Designing for visual appeal

Designing for Content

When creating the artifacts covered in this chapter, work from a completed content draft whenever possible. Working with "lorem ipsum" content is easy, but it can undermine the intent of a wireframe or prototype. In other words, fake content can lead to fake specifications.

Content boxes change size depending on what gets put into them by content management systems. Dynamic content fields can be filled with an image one day, copy the next, and a combination of the two on some other day. Having completed content helps designers plan for the appropriate amount of real estate necessary to execute interface functions.

Using this approach, wireframes and prototypes will contain real content which provides *context* to users, clients and testers as well as to designers creating these artifacts.

Designing for Technology

One of the questions that arises early in the discovery process of building or redesigning a site is: what devices do people actually use to access my site? If the project in question is a redesign, most website analytics packages can tell you how many users arrive at your site by desktop, mobile, or tablet.

Mobile browsing is increasing at a rapid rate, accounting for more than half of web traffic in some industries. Designing for a mobile experience is imperative, and can no longer be an afterthought. Provide mobile users with a top-notch site experience. Consider these two approaches:

- Build one site that works equally well on mobile, tablet, and desktop screens.
- Build two sites: one for mobile users and one for tablet and desktop users.

Building both a mobile and desktop/tablet optimized site can get expensive fast, plus having two separate sites means having to upload and test everything twice. Thus, it typically makes sense to take that approach only if your users need completely different experiences and real estate considerations are such that a responsive design solution won't work.

Let's take an example: American Airlines and Ideaction Corps, two vastly different companies with vastly different needs for mobile website support.

Figure 4.1 Desktop and mobile versions of the ideactioncorps.com.

Figure 4.2 Desktop and mobile versions of the aa.com.

Visitors who access the American Airlines web page on a desktop are primarily interested in searching for and booking flights, while visitors who access the AA page on a mobile device are primarily interested in checking into the flights they've already booked. These two experiences are so different that it made more sense to build two different sites.

By contrast, visitors to the site for Ideaction Corps, a general contractor for social impact projects, are interested in the same basic topics—submitting their project and learning about the organization—no matter which device they use to visit the site. As a result, their site was built to support responsive design so that their visitors would have an optimal experience independent of screen size.

Whichever approach you choose, the strategic aspects of mobile first design remain the same.

1. Context is key. Thinking about content for mobile users first helps you optimize for their needs first and progressively enhance the experience as the viewport grows.
2. Prioritizing site functions for mobile devices first will inform the entire design process and reframe discussions about usability, navigation, and so on. Multi-tap gestures are great for touchscreen smartphones, for instance, but how do you re-create that functionality in a desktop based mouse-and-keyboard environment?
3. Studies show that 74%[1] of consumers will wait a mere 5 seconds for a web page to load on their mobile device before abandoning the site. Because design elements like photos, videos, and animation are the chief drivers of longer download times, designing your site using a mobile first approach will drive design decisions that prioritize a quickly loading site.

Ultimately, designing your site's mobile interface first will ensure that its primary content, functionality and speed are prime drivers for all design decisions. This approach saves money, energy and time. To this end, your first decision is what web page layout is the best fit for your organization's core audiences.

Choosing a Website Layout Type

Web page layouts all fall in to one of three categories: fixed width, adaptive, and responsive.

Fixed-Width Layouts

Fixed-width layouts adhere to a pixel-perfect wrapper width that remains the same no matter what size screen the user is viewing the page on. Designers have maximum control over page layout, but fixed width layout doesn't allow for much flexibility on the part of the user if, for instance, they use a mobile device, a screen reader, or require large font sizes. Because they don't require multiple viewport sizes, fixed-width layouts can be a cost-effective option for your website, but they offer the worst user experience of the three types mentioned here.

Figure 4.3 Fixed-width layouts look the same no matter what size screen they are displayed on. people.com has a fixed-width layout, but it has been cleverly optimized for mobile users by creating a mobile-friendly menu layout on the far left of the screen.

Adaptive Layouts

Adaptive design begins with identifying the 2 to 5 most common screen sizes users are viewing your site with. Then, designers create a separate layout for each screen size. When a visitor arrives at the site, a piece of code detects what size device the user is viewing and serves up the layout that best matches the users screen size.

Figure 4.4 Adaptive layouts have designs to fit a pre-defined set of screen sizes.

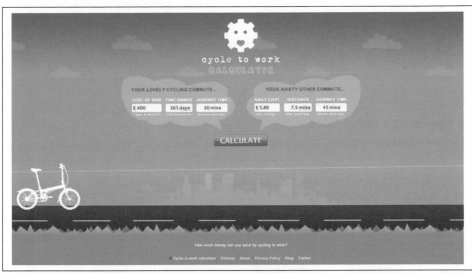

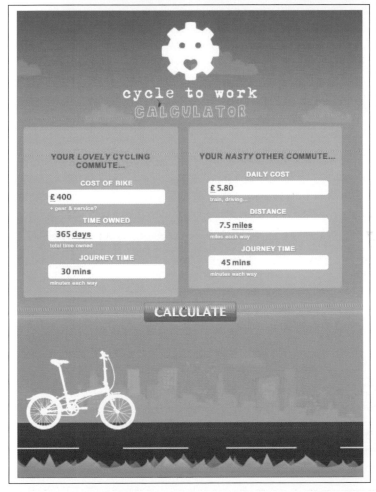

Figure 4.5 Responsive layouts adapt to any screen size.

Responsive Layouts

Responsive design layouts are based on a percentage-driven grid, which means that they can scale to any screen size without losing visual integrity. Unlike adaptive design layouts, which come in a set of predefined sizes, responsive designs can scale to fit any screen size. As a result, responsive design offers the best user experience across all devices. It is also generally the most time-consuming design option to implement.

When you are choosing which layout approach to take, base your decision on two factors: your audience needs and your budget. For many organizations, adaptive design offers the best balance between cost and user experience.

Designing For Usability

In their book *Web Design for ROI* (www.wd4roi.com), authors Lance Loveday and Sandra Niehaus cite "research has proven that visitors' ultimate likelihood to transact with an organization is heavily influenced by their experience with an organization's website." In other words, if your website is difficult to use people aren't going to use it.

We break down the design aspects of usability into three buckets:

1. Information Architecture
2. Interaction Design
3. Visual Design

Information Architecture

The Information Architecture Institute defines IA as "the art and science of organizing and labeling websites to support usability."[2] Its goal is to allow an audience to easily find and act on content you tailored to their needs and interests.

On a website, the most visible aspect of information architecture is the navigation bar on the homepage. You can learn a lot about an organization's digital strategy from the way they organize the content here.

Here's a screen shot of the homepage of Robinhood.org, a non-profit organization dedicated to fighting poverty in New York City.

Figure 4.6 The Robinhood.org homepage has a primary, secondary, and tertiary navigation.

The primary navigation options on their homepage are:

- The Problem
- Our Approach
- Our Impact
- Donate

Then, there's a secondary navigation in the upper left hand corner:

- About
- Programs
- News
- Initiatives
- Give

And finally, there's a tertiary navigation in the upper right hand corner:

- My Account
- Donate

Based on just those three navigation bars, we can draw several conclusions about Robinhood.org's website goals:

1. **The single most important goal for the Robinhood.org is to drive donations.** There is just one call to action on this homepage: Donate. There is a "donate" option in all three navigation bars and in the body of the homepage. It could not be more clear what Robinhood.org wants its visitors to do.

2. **Casual donors are the primary audience for this website.** The primary navigation is focused entirely on making a quick, data based case that casual visitors should choose Robinhood.org for their donation dollars.

3. **Donors interested in learning more about Robinhood.org are the secondary audience for this website.** The secondary navigation guides visitors to more in-depth information about how Robinhood.org operates, who they fund and their impact on the community.

4. **Members are the third most important audience for this website.** The tertiary navigation is dedicated to member accounts.

5. **People interested in getting funding from Robinhood.org are not an important audience for this website.** Information about how to get Robinhood.org funding is located in a sub-menu on the secondary navigation. Given the fact that this site has three main navigation bars, the fact that this information is buried in a sub-menu indicates that providing this information is not a top goal of the site.

Your information architecture informs design strategy by clearly identifying the top goals of the site and their calls to action. As you can see, Robinhood.org's designers used this information about the key goals and conversions of the site to highlight three out of four of the "Donate" calls to action in bright green. In addition, the body of the site is dominated by a single image (also called a hero image) that supports the goal of donation by showing the personal and emotional impact of their mission: a happy family eating a healthy meal.

Information Architecture and Site Maps

The core artifact of your website's information architecture is a site map. A site map is a diagram that shows every page that exists on a website (including the easy to forget things like error pages and forms) and how they connect to each other. They may start with sketches on whiteboards or cocktail napkins, but end up as tools for both humans and search engines to quickly interpret site content and structure. In their final form, they typically exist as HTML or XML documents in the root level directory of your website.

An HTML site map is like a table of contents for your website; it is the text version of your site navigation. As you can see from Orbit Media Studio's HTML site map below, the outline format gives users a quick bird's-eye view of all the content on your site in a visual hierarchy, which can help them quickly find the information they need.

Figure 4.7 Orbit Media Studio's site map, conveniently provided for users in HTML.

An XML site map is a list each of the URLs in a site along with metadata that tells search engines when each URL was last updated, how often it changes and how important it is compared to the other URLs on the site. Search engine web crawlers find sites and pages through links, so having an XML site map boosts your search engine rankings.

There are a range of services that generate XML site maps for you. Popular services include:

- XML-Sitemaps.com
- web-site-map.com
- xmlsitemapgenerator.org

These tools are great, but keep in mind that each time you add a piece of content to your website you also have to update the site map to keep everything current. Thankfully, most content management systems offer features or plug-ins to keep these files updated.

```
<?xml version="1.0" encoding="UTF-8"?>
<urlset xmlns="http://www.sitemaps.org/schemas/sitemap/0.9">
  <url>
    <loc>http://www.example.com/</loc>
    <lastmod>2005-01-01</lastmod>
    <changefreq>monthly</changefreq>
    <priority>0.8</priority>
  </url>
</urlset>
```

Figure 4.8 XML site maps need to be updated every time your content is.

Also, if you use Google's Webmaster Tools (and you should), it will want to know where your site map resides on the site, so it can assure repeat crawls of properly indexed site content.

This may sound like more engineering-speak than design strategy, but keep in mind that all of this data wrangling starts in the discovery phase of a website. Designers and content strategists have huge input here.

Information Architecture Exercises and Tools

Mapping out information architecture for a site project begins with understanding how potential users might attempt to access information on your site. There are several exercises and tools designers to gather this feedback and facilitate discussions with a team.

Wireframing

Think of wireframes as the blueprints for your website design. They're sketches of the basic structure and layout of elements you want on a web page. They can be precise, generated using wireframe or design software, or they can be simple, even sketched out on a napkin. The purpose of a wireframe is to visually map the way you want your website to function and where you want to put things on the page. We create wireframes before creating a full site design (and beginning development) because they're easy to sketch out and change while you gather consensus from stakeholders on how a page should look.

Here are some things that should inform your wireframing process:

- **Keep it high-level**. Wireframing doesn't need to get too detailed, especially in the beginning.
- **Don't be afraid to experiment with different layouts**. You're not committed to anything at this point, so be creative. Stick to general rules about where information should be placed, but think outside the box when it comes to elements like homepage design.
- **Use standard wireframing symbols**. To make sure your wireframes communicate correctly, use standard wireframing symbols like tabs, radio buttons, picture boxes, etc.
- **Use whatever layout program is easiest for you**. Wireframing is about getting thoughts on paper. If you literally need to use a pen and paper (and many designers recommend starting here), that's fine. Don't waste time learning a new tool before you start sketching.
- **Use your wireframes to start a conversation**. Wireframes are all about facilitating discussions with other stakeholders about how information should be presented on a site. They're not final designs, so be flexible and open minded to changes others might suggest.

Card Sorting

Card sorting is a user experience design technique designed to surface the way a website's visitors would naturally expect the site's content to be categorized. This insight into the expectations of your visitors helps you create a user-friendly information architecture for your future website. Typically, the higher the number of content elements, the greater the need for card sorting.

In a card sort exercise, every topic and type of content on a site gets written onto sticky notes and volunteers are invited to sort all the sticky notes so that similar topics and content types are grouped together and labeled. Each volunteer does their own sort and creates their own labels. The card sort facilitator records their organization, then scrambles up the notes again for the next participant to sort.

Once all the volunteers have completed the exercise, the card sort facilitator looks for patterns across all the sorts to find the biggest points of convergence and the biggest points of disagreement. The common groups are intuitive categories that can be used as the foundation of the site's information architecture and the outlier groups indicate areas for the UX team to focus on clarifying for users.

In order to conduct a card sort you need between one and two dozen site users who volunteer to help. It is absolutely necessary to recruit actual users who have not been involved in the design process, because you need insight into how people approach the site when they have no preconceived ideas about how it should work. Each volunteer will need about 15 to 30 minutes to complete the exercise. If you're having trouble recruiting volunteers, sweeten the pot by offering a freebie like a Starbucks gift card or a Ben & Jerry's coupon. Creating an intuitive information architecture is well worth the investment!

Once you've got your volunteers, explain to them that in this exercise they will be presented all of your website's content as "cards" and their job is to sort them into smaller categories that they think make sense, and label them. Tell them that if they can't decide where a card should go they should just leave it to the side.

Card sorting can be done with white boards and sticky notes or with software. If you use software, you can schedule your volunteers to sort simultaneously. If you run the exercise in person, you can conduct the sessions over the course of one day or several. Keep some coffee and cookies on hand, and try for a relaxing environment.

> ## Virtual Card Sorting Tools
>
> If sticky notes and recipe cards aren't your thing, there are plenty of software tools that can help you accomplish the same tasks. With card sorting software all your volunteers can do the exercise at the same time, and as an added bonus these services also make pattern analysis a snap. Here are a few:
>
> - Optimal Sort by Optimal Workshop: www.optimalworkshop.com/optimalsort.htm
> - WebSort by UX Punk: http://uxpunk.com/websort/
> - Simple Card Sort: www.simplecardsort.com/

When completed, be sure to thank the volunteers for helping and let them know they had an integral part in your website development process.

Card Sorting for Niles Public Library

Mightybytes conducted a card sorting exercise with patrons of Niles Public Library to help determine the appropriate navigation design for their website redesign. For our exercise we had 16 participants ranging from age 11 to 70 years old. 93% of our sample had previously used the library's website. All of them were real users of the current library website and patrons of the library's facility.

We used Optimal Sort to present our volunteers with over 100 cards depicting existing and planned site content, such as free events and information on youth services. The patrons were then responsible for sorting them into logical groups and then giving the groups names.

After the exercise was completed, Mightybytes merged any group names that were highly similar (for example, we merged "for kids" with the label "kids"), and began looking for patterns. Using Optimal Sort's dendograms (tree diagrams illustrating how cards were clustered within a hierarchy), similarity matrices (a type of spreadsheet that clusters the strongest card groups together), and the raw data, we were able to analyze how these patrons grouped library content in ways that made sense to them. Here are some of our key findings from our card sort;

1. Disagreements and challenges
   - **What is an eBook?**

Of 16 participants, eBooks was put into 15 different categories (94%). One may view this as highlighting the challenge of categorizing eBooks within a library website. While paper books have been around since the Fifth Dynasty, eBooks and the ubiquity of affordable devices to view them on have only been available as of the last dozen years or so. Additionally many people may not know that eBooks are available as a free library service, and may just associate these with Amazon purchases. Patrons asked themselves, is it media, part of book collections, related to electronics, or an online resource? Similarly, the card for "audio books" was categorized 14 different ways.

   - **Beyond traditional collections**

The role of a library within a community is complex. In addition to lending out books, music, and films, Niles Public Library also provides a wide array of essential services to their patrons. These include distributing free museum passes to families, distributing citizenship information, and even providing notary public service. There was no agreement on how to categorize these services.

It may be that these public service offerings fall under the radar of patrons who may not know that these services are offered, or that the results of our survey may have been colored by our small sample size. The challenge here is if very few people are looking for something, how can you ensure it's findable in a logical place?

   - **Is a library a brick and mortar location, or hub of services?**

Patrons struggled to understand how to categorize both the home delivery of books, and bookmobiles. This may indicate the possible misconception about the library being solely a physical, brick-and-mortar location versus the hub of an array of community services. The concept of a library being "mobile," or living outside the actual facility confused patrons.

Similarly, patrons created a number of different categories related to technology. These categories featured titles like "online," "technological," "computers and internet," and "computers and internet information," and the cards within those groups seemed to indicate a struggle to differentiate between virtual services available from remote locations (such as a patron's home or school), and the virtual services available to patrons at the brick-and-mortar library location. If anything, this highlighted the importance of educating patrons on the range of library services that are available to them in their own homes.

- **The problem with too much information**

When stuck patrons would often turn to the concept of "Information" as a category. This lead to "General Information," "Library Information," "Information," and "Info on the Library" being created as categories. None of these vague categories reached more than 59% agreement across our sample of patrons.

The main takeaway here is that the library should pursue valuable, understandable page names. Information as a category is too vague and subjective to be used on a website where you want to make things easy to find.

2. Similarities and Indicators

- **Age-specific content**

Age-specific content was grouped similarly by the majority of participants. Given the specificity of the content (for example "teen advisory board"), it was not hard for patrons to group these resources into natural categories. This proved our hypothesis that age-specific navigational destinations meet library patron's expectations and are easy to understand.

- **"My Account"**

The majority of patrons also paired and grouped similar items under "my account"; such as when their books are due, how to put an item on hold, and viewing item renewal policies. This clearly indicates that people want an easily accessible, single destination for all of the information regarding their own personal account with the library.

These insights from Niles Public Library's patrons had a big impact on our website information architecture design. As a result of these insights, we were able to create an intuitive interface that both helps patrons find what they are looking for quickly and easily and highlights some of the services that patrons may not be as aware of.

Tree Tests

Websites are organized in a hierarchy, or tree, of topics and subtopics that visitors navigate through to find what they need. Tree tests are a great way to test usability and the

Figure 4.9 As a result of the card sort, we created primary navigation categories with explicit labels like "using the library" rather than vaguer terms like "library information."

Here are some tree testing tools to help with site navigation design:

- Treejack (Optimalworkshop.com) lets you create a simplified site map to test.
- UserZoom (userzoom.com) is enterprise level software perfect for larger retail sites.
- C-Inspector (www.c-inspector.com) lets you upload your entire site map for testing.

"findability" of certain content types. If visitors can find site content within your hierarchy quickly and easily, there's a much higher chance the completed site will be successful. These exercises can go a long way to inform how to build out site maps and create organizational information hierarchies that make sense to the majority of users.

In a typical tree test, participants are tasked with locating a piece of information or content and then presented with a list of topics to choose from. When the participants chooses a topic they are presented with a list of subtopics. Participants continue choosing subtopics (and backtracking when necessary) until they find the topic that completes their task. In order for this exercise to be valuable, multiple potential users should complete the test.

Tree tests help answer a number of questions:

1. Can visitors find the task quickly and easily?
2. Where do visitors get lost and have to backtrack?

3. Do they have to stop and consider their choices, or do they make them quickly?
4. Overall, is the site hierarchy intuitive and easy to use?

Designing for Interaction

The goal of interaction design is to make it as simple and intuitive as possible for visitors to take action on your site. This not only includes the primary and secondary navigation schemes but also the blog, shopping cart checkout process, contact and support forms, social media integration, and any other potential areas where content and the successful dissemination of site information could get in the way of seamless user experiences. The smoothness of these interactions can be the difference between your visitors taking action through your site or finding another option.

Creating user stories and mapping user task flows in your design strategy sessions will help ensure that your designers are clear on how the site should work.

User Stories

Developing user stories is a process taken from agile programming in which the site or app is defined in terms of all the potential actions users could take on the site. User stories are written in the following format: "As an X, I want to do Y in order to achieve Z."

For example, a set of blog user stories might be:

- As a writer for this blog, I want to create an author profile so readers know who wrote my post.
- As a reader of this blog, I want to comment on this post to share my views.
- As the administrator of this blog, I want to tag each post so blog topics are easy to find.

The ultimate goal of defining a site by a series of user stories is to ensure that every function that's built into the site delivers a benefit to the site's users. Developers derive their technical specifications from user stories, content creators use them to determine what kind of content best serves each desired function and designers use them to create intuitive layouts and interfaces.

User Task Flows

A user task flow is the path a visitor follows through a web interface to accomplish the task named in a user story. User task flows are the core of digital design because they prompt every member of the team to think critically about how to design a site to help visitors achieve each goal in as few steps as possible no matter how they accessed the site.

For example, let's take the following simple user story: "As a potential home buyer, I want to find a rent calculator so that I can decide if taking on a mortgage is cheaper than renting."

Your next task is to design a set of user flows that make it as easy as possible for your visitors to reach the mortgage calculator on your site. Three common entry points are:

1. Search result for "mortgage calculator"
2. Link in an ad for "mortgage calculator"
3. Home page

The user flows starting from these entry points might be:

Figure 4.10 A mortgage calculator user task flow.

Designers would then use these flows to influence the layout and user interface of each page in the path. Of course, this is a simple example; the real challenge is designing for stacked user flows. For example, once someone uses the mortgage calculator what are their next steps?

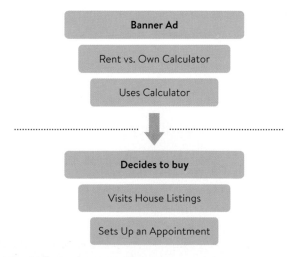

Figure 4.11 Stacked user flows shows workflow between multiple tasks.

Stacked user flows show interaction designers which options they should build into the mortgage calculator workflow to help visitors get to their next step. The layout of the mortgage calculator results page based on the stacked user flow might ultimately look like this:

Figure 4.12 The layout of the mortgage calculator based on the stacked user flows.

User Task Flow Mapping Exercise

Mapping out all the interactions your users will have with your site is too big a task for one person. This exercise is an efficient way to capture and organize all the necessary user tasks. Plan on dedicating 2–3 hours to this session. Keep your working group small (4–5 people, if possible) and be sure each person participating has an overall understanding of the product or website being built.

1. Write out each task a user must accomplish. Be specific and add one task per sticky note. Start each with a verb (i.e., *Compose* message, etc.). Put all on a whiteboard and remove duplicates. These are **user tasks.**
2. Group tasks similar to each other closer together; move those dissimilar from each other further apart on a whiteboard.
3. Place grouped tasks, one after the other, from left to right on a whiteboard in the order which a user might accomplish them (left-to-right progression is meant to indicate time).
4. Name each set of tasks across the top to form columns of activities from left to right, again in the order they might be undertaken. These are **user activities.**

5. Add sub-steps of each task moving vertically down under each step. These are your **user stories** and can sometimes get lengthy (have plenty of stickies on hand).

6. Walk through the skeleton of user activities you have created. Are there categories you can merge or delete? Is anything missing? Can you remove steps in each process? What would be most intuitive for users?

7. Draw connections with arrows or lines between your boxes. Include both linear and non-linear user paths through the site.

Bonus: You can also start fleshing out ideas for which features will be included in release one, which are saved for release two or three and so on. Did we mention that your website is never done?

Pro tip: Using different color sticky notes for user tasks, activities and stories can be quite helpful to quickly identify the informational hierarchy presented in story mapping exercises.

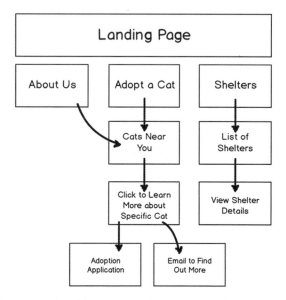

Figure 4.13 User flow maps should be captured so you can refer to them throughout your project process when discussing strategy. Your user flow map will be incredibly useful later in the process when your team tackles:

- **Identifying** new content needs driven by the design, like supporting copy and images for calls to action.
- **Mapping** interactive design elevments like page layouts and wireframes.
- **Planning** visual design elements like supporting imagery, graphics and calls-to-action.
- **Defining** goals and funnels in analytics programs.

Designing for Visual Appeal

Building page layouts that support the structure of your content and provide a natural visual hierarchy increases conversion rates as well as the site's "stickiness." Your site's most valuable propositions should be immediately apparent upon page load, so make them blindingly easy to find. Don't leave any room for interpretation or any question in a user's mind regarding how to interact with your site. For example, here is the home page of People for Bikes, an organization dedicated to advocating for all cyclists. Their number one goal for visitors? Tell us your story about biking. Clear, simple and engaging.

Figure 4.14 Don't be shy about telling people exactly what you'd like them to do.

Here are a few strategic rules of thumb to keep in mind when planning out your site's visual design.

The Gutenberg Rule

The Gutenberg Rule is a model that describes how readers scan a page. In Western cultures, readers' eyes go straight to the upper left hand corner, then look towards the bottom right. The upper right hand captures the next level of attention, with the bottom left being the least noticed.

When designing for the Gutenberg Rule, put important benefits-driven header text and (if applicable) a call-to-action button in the primary optical area, where they will be viewed first and provide a natural lead-in to the page's content.

By default, a reader's eyes will end up in the terminal area at the bottom right of your page. Put action items such as purchase call-outs, form lead-ins, and invitations to learn more in this area. Remember to make the buttons obvious and the text an easy indicator of what to do next.

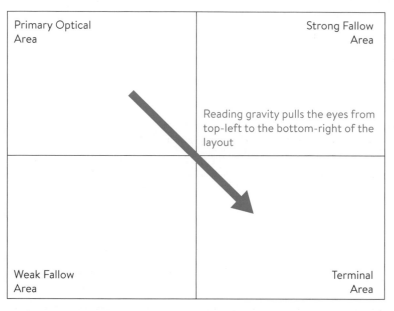

Figure 4.15 and 4.16 The Gutenberg Rule in a diagram and applied to a web page.

Color Palette

Devising an effective color palette is usually one of the first steps toward building out a site's overall aesthetic look and feel. It is also one of the most important.

Here are a few suggestions for making good use of color on your site:

- Use colors relevant to your industry.
- Consider potential cultural implications of color choices.

- Avoid using color as the only source of important data.
- Consider neutral backgrounds for content-heavy sites.
- Site sections can be delineated by color use.
- Light type on dark backgrounds is often difficult to read.

Readability

Choosing type elements that support your awesome layout is of course an important part of the design process. Of equal relevance is the readability of your type. Here are a few quick guidelines for insuring maximum readability:

- Use font sizes appropriate for maximum readability, keeping in mind that the user can change this preference at any time, which could have an impact on your layout.
- Maintain high contrast between background and text colors.
- Use bulleted lists, introductory summaries, clear titles, and stand-alone chunks to facilitate scanning.

Image vs. Text

While the visual impact of image-driven buttons can sometimes offer a better-looking navigation system, what you make up for in attractiveness you lose in optimization options. Whenever possible, make your buttons text and use CSS to style them. Here's why:

- Search engines can't interpret images, which means text in images hurts your search engine optimization.
- Screen readers can't read images, which means your site won't be as accessible to people with disabilities.
- Styled text is easy to update using a keyboard; images have to be created and individually uploaded.

Design Conventions

Over decades of web surfing, people have come to expect websites to follow certain rules, including:

- The logo of the organization in the top left
- A search function in the top right
- The primary navigation at the top of the page
- Contact information in the footer
- Submenus on the left

While not every website must follow these conventions, following them will make it easier for people to use your site, which is your primary goal. Save your innovative ideas for content, not overhauling the interface.

Here are three sites: (Red), Alliance for African Assistance, and Dreamentia. These three sites follow some of these rules and break others. What do you think works and doesn't work?

Figure 4.17

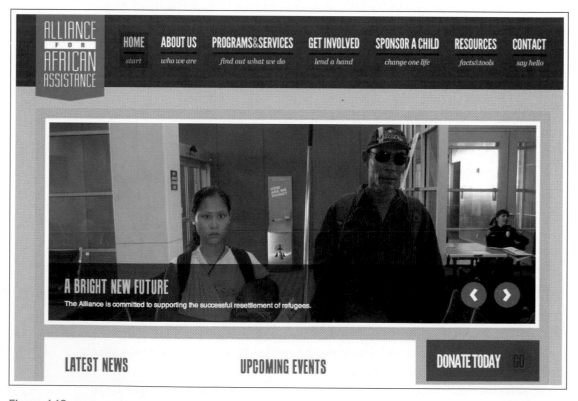

Figure 4.18

Figure 4.19 Which conventional rules are being followed and which are being broken on these three sites?

Content, Not Ads

People tend to have common expectations regarding what constitutes a banner ad. Ads are often punctuated by animation in somewhat standardized sizes (skyscrapers, banners, buttons, rectangular pop-ups, crawls along the bottom of mobile apps, and so on). With that in mind, don't design critical page information that looks or functions like advertising. Not only could it be off-putting (and confusing) to users, but it undermines the importance of what you have to say as well. Calls-to-action are great, but if you insert them after every paragraph or give them pop-up functions, you undermine the possibility of your content performing to its full potential.

Visual Design Exercise

Ask your internal stakeholders in the design process to find 3 to 5 sites that they like. Find a space where you can display the sites so that everyone can see them. Hold a meeting in which all your stakeholders view the sites as a team and talk through what they like and don't like about them. The final site should be your current site (if you have one) so people can discuss how some of the popular design elements you just identified could be utilized in a redesign.

For more in-depth information about implementing good visual design, go to Chapter 8.

Conclusion

In this chapter, we discussed how design strategy should support business goals by making it easy for visitors to find and use content on a website. What we covered:

- Digital design is about how a site or application works, not just how it looks.
- Mobile First as an important design strategy for creating sites that work across the widest array of devices and platforms possible.
- Principles of information architecture, interactive design and visual design to guide your design strategy sessions.

Profile

Figure 4.20 Russ Unger, Experience Design Director

Russ Unger

Russ Unger is an Experience Design Director in Chicago where he leads teams and projects in design and research. He is co-author of the book *A Project Guide to UX Design, Designing the Conversation, and Speaker Camp* for Peachpit Press (Voices That Matter). Russ is also working on a book on guerrilla design and research methods that is due out, well, sometime.

Russ is co-founder of ChicagoCamps, which hosts high-value technology events in the Chicago area, and he is also on the Advisory Board for the Department of Web Design and Development at Harrington College of Design.

Russ has two daughters who both draw better than he does and are currently beginning to surpass his limited abilities in coding.

If there was one single UX task, concept, idea that you think marketers should embrace what would it be?

Observe your customers in their natural environments–be that work, home, wherever it is that they do the whatever it is that they do with the thing that you are marketing to them–and watch them use your product. There is nothing more magical than that simple observation in a very normal, natural environment to help you gain insight into what is working, what isn't working, and how your product is being used in ways you never imagined.

Then, repeat it with more customers. And repeat it every time you think you need to change something, and after you've changed something. Doing this with your family, significant others, children, parents, as subjects don't count. And you don't count, either—you're not the user.

How do you convince customers who don't think they need UX or don't have the budget for UX to give it a try?

To some degree, I don't. Don't get me wrong—I think everyone should invest in their user experience efforts, and more and more organizations are starting to lock into the value of UX. Those are the organizations I want to work with—and sure, some will have varying degrees of acceptance and resistance, of course. If someone doesn't believe in observing, listening and talking to their customers, they're not really allowing someone in UX to be successful anyway, and it takes that realization to really get some traction.

Notes

1. HubSpot "23 Eye-Opening Mobile Marketing Stats You Should Know," June 21, 2012, http://blog.hubspot.com/blog/tabid/6307/bid/33314/23-Eye-Opening-Mobile-Marketing-Stats-You-Should-Know.aspx
2. Information Architecture Institute, "What Is Information Architecture," www.iainstitute.org/documents/learn/What_is_IA.pdf

CHAPTER FIVE

Measurement Strategy

Measuring content campaign effectiveness will help you make data-driven decisions about what's working and what's not. This will save you time, money, and resources on campaigns that underperform while iterating to improve those that do. Your measurement strategy should focus on metrics that show whether or not you're actually achieving the goals laid out in your Content Strategy Framework and *ignoring the rest*.

The art of wresting actionable insights from analytics can be overwhelming, largely because interpretation depends so heavily on an individual organization's unique goals. In this chapter, we'll:

- Provide an overview of analytics basics.
- Lay out some general principles for identifying the best metrics for your organization.
- Define a three-step process for identifying Key Performance Indicators (KPIs).
- Explore special considerations for social and mobile metrics.
- Outline a strategy for benchmarking your measurement efforts.
- Discuss iterating your content based on your measurement strategy.

Analytics Basics

Analytics tools can be configured to capture truly awe-inspiring amounts of data, so use the strategy document you created in Chapter 1 to narrow your focus to the metrics that provide actionable insight for your organization. Many important content marketing metrics tend to fall into one of four categories: visitors, content, design and promotion. While the exact report names vary depending on which analytics service you use, the information you can track is substantially consistent across systems.

1. Visitors

Your visitors are all the people who land on your site, and there are four things you should try to find out about them:

1. How did they find us?

The Traffic Sources report will tell you all sorts of information about where visitors to your site are coming from, including:

- **Overview:** General information on traffic sources.
- **Direct Traffic:** Visitors who came directly to your site without a referring link or search engine.
- **Referring Sites:** Sites that referred visitors to your site.
- **Social:** Social media channels that are referring visitors to your site.
- **Search Engines:** Which search engines sent how many visitors to your site?
- **All Traffic Sources:** A breakdown of each source referring traffic to your site.

2. How often do they visit us?

The Audience report will tell you the number of times people visit your site, how recently they did so, and the length and depth of their visits. You can also figure out what percentage of your audience is new and what percentage is made up of return visitors.

3. Where do they live?

The Audience report also captures the countries that your visitors come from and the primary language used by their browser. This information can help you figure out how well your efforts to communicate in different languages are working.

4. What devices are they using?

Analytics tools can break down everything from browsers, OS, number of screen colors and resolution, which version of Flash visitors have, and whether or not their browser supports Java. You can also figure out what percentage of your audience is accessing your site on mobile, which will help you make decisions about mobile sites and optimization.

2. Promotion

There are three types of metrics that show you how well your efforts to promote your content are working:

- **Keywords:** Track which keywords send traffic to your site, and which don't.
- **Campaigns:** Effective campaigns will drive traffic to your site. Tracking ad campaign referral traffic enables you to assess both how effective individual campaigns are and to compare multiple campaigns.
- **Ad Versions:** This feature shows you which versions of what ads sent traffic to your site, which makes it a handy A/B testing tool for ad effectiveness.

3. Content

Content performance reports provide a wealth of information based on how users interact with the content on your site, including:

Web Analytics Software

Web analytics software is designed to help you answer important strategic questions, such as:

- Are potential customers engaging with my website in actionable ways that drive conversions? Why or why not?
- Which site content/pages perform best? Which have room for improvement?
- Can my site conversion rate be improved? If so, how?

These questions likely came up during early strategy sessions when you defined KPIs, targets and objectives. Web tracking and analytics software should help you answer them and provide a roadmap for improvement over time.

Analytics Tools

Because Google Analytics (now Universal Analytics) is easy to install, provides a wealth of data, and doesn't cost a dime it is a popular option for organizations that are just beginning to develop an analytics strategy. It's not the only option, however. Here are some popular analytics software packages:

- **Kissmetrics:** Customer tracking software that connects content with sales. http://kissmetrics.com
- **Crazy Egg:** Eye-tracking SaaS package that tracks user behavior through heatmaps, scrollmaps, and click-throughs. http://crazyegg.com
- **Adobe Marketing Cloud:** Formerly known as Omniture, AMC is the top of the line tool for measuring all your digital efforts, not just your website. www.adobe.com/solutions/digital-marketing.html
- **Piwik:** An open source PHP/MySQL analytics application that has a plug-in architecture for extending capabilities. http://piwik.org/
- **Grape Web Statistics:** Simple, open-source tool geared toward web developers. www.quate.net/grape
- **Snoop:** A desktop-based analytics application. http://report.reinvigorate.net/snoop

- **Content by Popularity:** Pages organized in order from most viewed to least.
- **Content by Title:** Page titles in order from most viewed to least.
- **Content Drilldown:** Visitor paths through site, including time on pages, whether or not they exited on a specific page, and if the page generated any income.
- **Page View:** Page view metrics tend to be given a lot of weight when measuring how a site performs. In reality, it simply represents a viewed page. In some cases, such as a "thank you" page that appears after filling out a form or purchasing a product, it has the potential to represent a certain level of engagement, but, for the most part, it simply means a page has been landed upon, nothing more.

4. Design

Design metrics show you how easy it is for your visitors to take action through your site. Key design metrics include:

- **Site Search:** Track what visitors search for, which results pages they go to, where they began their searches, and so on. This information can help you assess your site design and organization. For example, if a topic is frequently searched you might decide to reorganize your content to make that topic easier for visitors to find.
- **Bounce Rate:** Your bounce rate measures the number of visitors who land on a page of your site and leave without ever going to another page. The higher this number, the more effort you should consider putting into increasing site engagement. If 75% of your visitors check out a page on your blog and then leave, perhaps you should think about ways of potentially engaging them further through things like "Related Posts" or specific calls-to-action that lead them further into a conversion funnel.
- **Top Landing Pages:** The list of pages where visitors entered the site.
- **Top Exit Pages:** The list of pages where visitors exited the site.

- **Site Overlay:** An overlay of your home page with percentage values for where users clicked.

Choosing Performance Metrics

You have *many* metrics to choose from. Choosing which ones are right for your organization is a matter of understanding your high-level objectives, creating a hypothesis around what types of content will help achieve those objectives, then publishing and measuring that content. That's a lot to keep straight, but the Content Strategy and Marketing Metrics model we introduced in Chapter 1 will help.

Your performance metrics should answer the question, "Did this content effectively move the needle for our organization?" If yes, you should continue on with it. If not, consider a new campaign.

One way to conceptualize the overarching plan for measuring content and digital marketing efforts is this cycle:

- **Yahoo! Web Analytics:** Yahoo's alternative to Universal Analytics. http://web.analytics.yahoo.com/
- **WebTrends:** An enterprise-wide analytics solution meant for large sites. www.webtrends.com/
- **4Q:** A surveying application focused on improving your traditional numerical Web analytics by supplementing it with actual user feedback. http://4q.iperceptions.com/

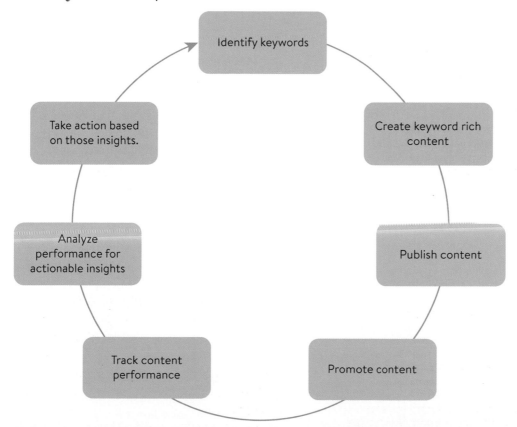

Figure 5.1 The ultimate goal of tracking performance metrics is to identify actionable steps to take to improve your content.

Connecting content strategy to actionable metrics can be tricky if you're not used to looking at data on a regular basis, so let's explore four principles for making informed analytics decisions:

1. Flat vs. Actionable
2. Company vs. Competitive
3. Aggregate vs. Segmented
4. Trends vs. Spikes

1. Flat vs. Actionable Metrics

Flat metrics require context to be useful, but actionable metrics show whether or not you're meeting goals, can help you map out a path to improvement, and are highly correlated with ROI. Here are some examples of each:

Flat	Actionable
Twitter followers	Shares by tweet content
Page views	Page views per new and returning customers
Facebook followers	Shares by Facebook content
Subscribers	Click-throughs
Registered users	Current active users

Impressions and Vanity Metrics

Flat metrics are also often known as "vanity" metrics because if they are presented with no context, they can give the impression that your efforts are successful, even though they don't actually measure your progress toward meeting goals.

Impressions are a great example of a vanity metric. In digital marketing parlance, impressions are the aggregate number of potential views based on the followers of your followers (or friends, connections, etc.). As you can imagine, impression numbers could very quickly grow in to tens of thousands or even millions of potential viewers for a piece of content.

But for the total impressions number to be meaningful, every friend of every friend you have on a given social network would have to be looking at their news feed and/or sharing your content at precisely the same time. And we all know that's not happening. While impressions provide general context for the potential reach of a piece of content, they don't reflect reality.

The key difference between the two is that the actionable metrics suggest a course of, well, action. For example, knowing that you have 10,000 page likes on Facebook is less useful than knowing that Facebook status updates with images get re-shared four times as often as Facebook status updates with just text. Here's another example: let's say your company has 500 Facebook likes. That number is meaningless unless you know that your peers have 50–100 likes. Even with that context, you don't have any information about whether or not you should work to increase your Facebook likes or not. Just because your content may show up in someone's news feed doesn't necessarily mean it will add enough value to incite them to take a conversion-driven action of some sort.

So in other words, while it might be great that your brand page has 5,000 likes on Facebook, it means little if your competitors all have 20,000 likes. And it means even less if none of those 5,000 interact with your page in meaningful ways.

2. Company vs. Peer Metrics

The metrics you gather on your own company become even more useful when you compare them to your peers. Analyzing your metrics in the context of others helps you in three ways:

- It enables you to benchmark your efforts against others and set practical targets for improvement.
- It helps you take advantage of others' research and experience.
- It helps you identify opportunities to differentiate your digital strategy.

Peer Metrics Chart

Here is an example of the peer metrics our imaginary organization, Roadshare Chicago, would track for its fellow imaginary organizations Share the Road and Rollerblade for the Environment.

There are two types of information you can glean from peer analysis. The first is how others use digital platforms to increase brand awareness, which will give you a benchmark to shoot for. The second is finding channels where others don't perform well.

Social Media Presence	Roadshare Chicago	Share the Road	Rollerblade for the Environment
Google+	159	840	Not in top 50
Facebook	1,846	10,478	325
Instagram	122	988	Not in top 50
Twitter	2,455	8,210	940
Vine	66	Not in top 50	Not in top 50

Keyword Ranking	Roadshare Chicago	Share the Road	Rollerblade for the Environment
Chicago bike lanes	5th	2nd	Not in top 50
Bike lane petitions	4th	22nd	Not in top 50
Chicago bicycle law	2nd	1st	Not in top 50
Chicago cycling statistics	4th	2nd	Not in top 50

Overall Content Performance	Roadshare Chicago	Share the Road	Rollerblade for the Environment
Blog frequency	2x/week	2-3x/week	1x/month
Alexa bounce rate	64.70%	43.30%	69.20%
Top keywords	Chicago lakefront path	Chicago cyclist	rollerblade derby workout

Overall site Performance			
	Roadshare Chicago	Share the Road	Rollerblade for the Environment
Google page speed	67 mobile, 78 desktop	78 mobile, 91 desktop	57 mobile, 72 desktop
Mobile optimized?	Yes	Yes	No
Usability score	Easy	Easy	Medium

Figure 5.2 Comparing metrics across these organizations clearly shows that Share the Road has both built a more robust social following than the other two organizations and has a better SEO strategy.

3. Aggregate vs. Segmented Metrics

The aggregated data you see when you crack open an analytics dashboard is just the jumping off point. The really useful information is found by slicing your data into segments. For example, the total number of page visits for your blog doesn't tell you very much on its own, but discovering that 20% of your visits come from mobile phone users in Mexico suggests some follow up analysis and action.

Here are some metrics to consider segmenting:

Traffic

The easiest place to begin tackling segmented data is with your traffic sources. What percentage of your traffic comes from search vs. direct? How about mobile vs. desktop? What percentage comes from social media, and within the social media segment which platforms drive the most traffic? Segmenting by traffic sources tells you a lot about who your visitors are and how they access your site. For example, a low percentage of traffic from search suggests that your SEO strategy could use some fine-tuning. A high percentage of traffic from mobile devices coupled with a high bounce rate might suggest that you should devote some energy to mobile optimization.

Page Visits

When you're looking at your organization's traffic patterns, the key question is "do visitors who take an action I want them to take (subscribe, donate, buy) visit different parts of the site than visitors who don't?" For example, an analysis of the pages visited by people who request a free trial might show that 80% watched a demo video—good information to have as you allocate your content creation budget.

Figure 5.3 This is a report of Mightybytes' traffic sources over the course of one month. As you can see, the bulk of our traffic comes from organic search because we spend so much time creating and optimizing good content.

Questions to ask yourself as you dig into your page visits include:

- Which pages do visitors spend the most time on?
- Do those pages play a critical role in your overall conversion strategy?
- If so, where do they fall in the conversion funnel?
  - Top = brand awareness
  - Middle = education
  - Bottom = conversion
- If not, what purpose do they serve?
- Are there pages you want people to visit that aren't getting much traffic?

Another useful thing to check with page visits is where people go from your popular pages, and traffic visualization reports can show you. For example, this is a report showing the behavior of people who visited one of our most popular blog posts, a piece on digital prototypes by Stephanie Daniels, one of our developers. As you can see, most people found this piece through a Google search. Once these visitors read the post, most of them left, but the handful of people who stayed on the site clicked through to a few different places, including Stephanie's bio, to our home page, and to other blog posts.

Figure 5.4 This is a report on the visited pages on mightybytes.com. As you can see, one of our most popular pages is a "how-to" on creating a DIY photo booth, a cool subject but one that has absolutely nothing to do with our core business. The DIY photo booth post is a constant reminder to us to create content that's in alignment with our business goals!

This report tells us that people who visit this post are interested in learning a new skill from us rather than hiring us—at least immediately. If this pattern holds across our most popular blog posts, then we might conclude that the best call to action for our blog would be "sign up for our newsletter" rather than "got a project? Contact us."

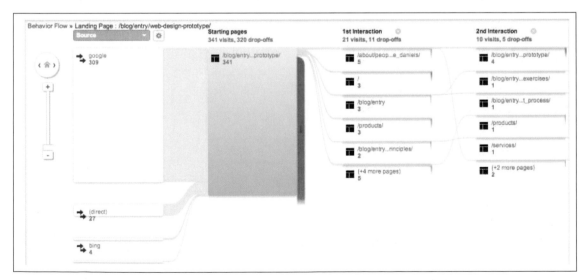

Figure 5.5 This report shows where visitors to one of our most popular blog posts go when they're done reading.

4. Trends vs. Spikes

Trends tell you how well your overall strategy is working, while spikes can tell you the impact of individual events or tactics. For example, if your organization hosts a blog, your goal might be to grow your audience over time. You would look to spikes in visitors to identify what specific blog post topics drive the most traffic.

The challenge is to separate out popular blog posts that grow your audience over the long term from popular blog posts that don't drive visitors to other content on your site.

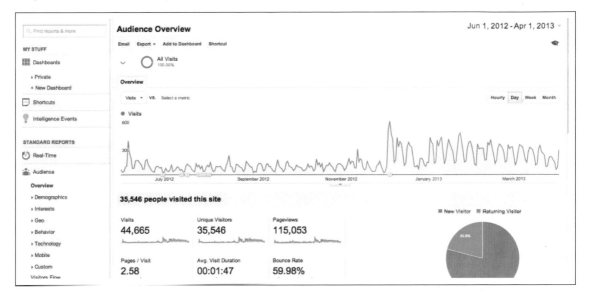

Figure 5.6 If you've got spikes in traffic paired with overall growth, then you are doing your job right.

Key Performance Indicators

KPIs, or key performance indicators, do precisely what they say: they indicate whether or not an initiative is succeeding in its goal. KPIs are different for every industry and often unique to a marketing campaign. They can be as far-reaching as amount of increased revenue or as granular as number of "likes" on Facebook within a given time period.

This is our three step process to identify KPIs:

1. **Understand the business or organizational goals.** What is your business or organization hoping to achieve this year? Use these objectives as a starting point for creating your campaigns. How can marketing assist in moving the needle?

Validated Learning

A concept popular in lean and agile software development, validated learning is useful to the online marketer as well. Through rapid development cycles called "sprints" designers and programmers build the minimum functionality necessary to prove a hypothesis. That functionality is then tested with real world users and the results measured. Once the hypothesis has been proven (or disproven), the team evaluates what they learned and can make educated decisions based on data about what next steps should be. Many web apps are built this way and it's a pretty standard method of "growth hacking" a digital startup.

What does this have to do with content marketing? Marketers and community managers can take the same approach with their content campaigns. By running A/B or multivariate tests and tracking performance data or conversion funnel success rates, you can quickly test the efficacy of design and content-related decisions. This will validate whether or not your efforts are worth continuing to pursue. For more information on validated learning and making metrics-based business,

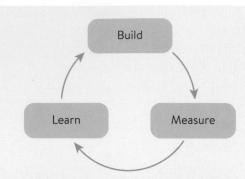

Figure 5.7 By measuring hypothesis validation, product developers can make educated decisions regarding whether to abandon their hypothesis (pivot) or stay the course (persevere).

marketing, and design decisions, check out these great books:

- *The Lean Startup* by Eric Ries (http://theleanstartup.com/)
- *Growth Hacker Marketing* by Ryan Holiday (www.amazon.com/Growth-Hacker-Marketing-Advertising-ebook/dp/B00BPDR3JM)
- *UX for Lean Startups* by Laura Klein (www.amazon.com/UX-Lean-Startups-Experience-ebooks/dp/B00CMFJZ1Q/)
- *Lean Analytics* by Benjamin Yoskovitz and Alistair Croll (www.amazon.com/Lean-Analytics-Startup-OReilly-ebook/B00AG66LTM/0
- *A/B Testing* by Dan Siroker and Pete Koomen (www.amazon.com/Testing-Powerful-Clicks-Customers-ebook/dp/B00E1JO50M/)

2. **Plan campaigns you believe will help achieve business/organizational goals.** Now that you know what the business hopes to achieve this year, what kind of marketing campaigns can you create that will help reach those objectives?

3. **Decide which metrics will effectively measure the success of your campaign.** Once you've brainstormed ideas for marketing campaigns you think can help achieve organizational goals, decide which actionable metrics you'll use to determine whether or not each campaign is successful. These are your KPIs.

To give you an idea of what other organizations use to measure success, Figure 5.7 is a handy, dandy cheat sheet with a set of common KPIs.

Once you have defined measurable metrics that might be worthwhile to your organization, it's time to slash and burn. Whittle your list down to a handful of metrics that will:

1. Help you understand whether or not you're meeting your goal, and

2. Help you decide what to do next.

Acquisition	Cost per acquisition of new customer/visitor
	Click-through rate for ads and emails
	% New vs. returning visitors
Behavior	Bounce rate (A low bounce rate shows you've promoted your content/product correctly and visitors are finding what they expect to find)
	Page depth (Engaged visitors will visit more pages in a single visit)
	Visitor loyalty (A high rate of visitor loyalty shows that your visitors find enough value in your site to come back over and over)
	Task completion (Are visitors able to do what they came to your site to do)
	Checkout abandonment rate
Outcomes	Conversion rates on macro and micro goals
	Days to conversion
	% Assisted conversions (measures all the touch points a visitor experienced before converting on a goal)

Figure 5.8 Common and useful Key Performance Indicators

Here is a simple rule to remember: if a metric doesn't supply you with actionable data, it is not a KPI. From your whittled down list, choose the one metric that matters most and make that your golden ring.

KPI Resources

Here are some resources to help you identify organizational KPIs:

- Kaushik.net
- SmartKPIs.com
- SimpleKPI.com

Configuring Goals and Funnels

Once you've identified your KPIs, you can set up any goals and funnels necessary for your analytics software to track your KPI performance.

Goals

In Google Analytics, now Universal Analytics, a goal represents a user action or engagement with your website that is important to the success of your business. Goal conversions are the primary metric for measuring how well your website fulfills business and marketing objectives. E-commerce sites could have goals for completed transactions or visitors entering the shopping system. Non-e-commerce websites might have goals like downloading a document, completing a contact request form, viewing specific pages, or adding/editing a profile. Once you have set up these goals, you will be able to see conversion rates and the monetary value of the visitors that come to your website and track improvement on them over time.

Three common goals include:

- Time on Site
- Pages per Visit
- URL Destination

For all three types of goals you can enter a goal value then measure how it performs. Universal Analytics uses this assigned goal value to calculate return on investment (ROI) and other return-related metrics for non-e-commerce sites whenever a goal is successfully reached by site users. Measuring improvement (or lack thereof) on these values can help validate decisions regarding whether or not to continue with that particular web-based content marketing strategy.

1. Time on Site

A conversion (i.e., goal being met) is triggered when a visitor spends more or less time on the site than the threshold you have specified. It can be difficult to determine what that threshold is, however. What is the right amount of time that qualifies as a quality visit? This really depends on the goals of your site.

Let's say you just started a non-profit organization and are looking to build awareness around a cause, such as improving patient care in healthcare. Assuming your website is designed and built as a place where you want people to spend time consuming content and learning about your mission, you might want to track how much time visitors spend on your site. An increase in the amount of time a visitor spends on your site could indicate a higher level of engagement with your content and an increased knowledge of and interest in your cause. Or it could mean they are lost.

2. Pages per Visit

A conversion is triggered when a visitor views more pages or fewer pages than the threshold you have specified. Again, you have to decide how many pages per visit is considered valuable to your business goals. More pages doesn't necessarily equate to more value. It could mean that users are having a difficult time finding what they need. Or it could mean that they came to your site, made a purchase, then left.

3. URL Destination

This is probably the most popular and valuable goal type, as it can be configured to correlate with specific calls-to-action that you set. A URL Destination goal is the page visitors see once they have completed an activity (i.e., met a goal). For example, a site that requires registration might define this destination as the "Thank You for signing up" page after the user has completed registration. This goal triggers a conversion when a visitor views the page you have specified as the destination.

Before you enter the URL Destination value, you need to choose a Match Type. The Match Type defines how Universal Analytics will identify a URL for either a goal or a funnel. There are three Match Types to choose from:

- **Exact Match:** This is an identical match on every character in the URL of the page you want to define.
- **Head Match:** This matches identical characters starting at the beginning of the specified URL string up to and including the last character of the string. Use this match if the beginning of your URL Destination is constant (the Head) but is followed by various unique session identifiers or other query parameters.
- **Regular Expression Match:** This uses special characters to enable wildcard and flexible matching, useful when the head of the URL, query parameters, or both can vary between users.

After choosing the Match Type, you need to enter the request Uniform Resource Identifier of the URL destination that a user reaches once they have completed the specific task. So if your goal page is "www.mysite.com/thankyou.html" you would enter "/thankyou.html".

The last detail to enter for the URL Destination goal is a Goal Value. This step is optional.

Funnels

If users need to navigate through several pages to reach the page you would like them to view, you can set up a URL Destination as a goal for your site. Additionally, you have the option to define a "funnel path" for each goal. A funnel path is a set of pages you expect visitors to view on their way to completing the conversion. For example, a big box retailer might have a "complete a purchase funnel" made up of the following steps: viewing a product category page, viewing a product page, viewing a shopping cart, adding a product, checking out, making payment, etc., etc.

Universal Analytics features some powerful visual features that can show you how the funnel path of your site performs. Universal Analytics creates a Funnel Visualization report that tells you how many visitors entered and exited each step of the funnel as well as where they came from and where they went.

You may enter up to 10-page URLs in a single funnel. Remember these pages represent the path you expect visitors to take on their way to reaching the specified goal. The final goal page should not be included as a funnel step, however.

The URLs you enter must not contain the domain name. Therefore, if "www.mysite.com/step1.html" is a page in the funnel path you would enter "/step1.html." Give each funnel URL a meaningful name to make the Funnel Visualization report easy to understand.

There is a check box labeled "Required Step" next to the first funnel step. If this box is checked, users reaching your goal page without going through this funnel page will not be counted as conversions in the Funnel Visualization report.

Universal Analytics will use the same match type you selected for the URL Destination in the funnel configuration. Be sure to check your funnel URLs for accuracy.

Social Media Campaign Measurement Strategies

In addition to your website's performance metrics, you'll also track the performance of each social media campaign you undertake. A simplified version of the framework we introduced in Chapter 1 will help you ensure that each digital campaign is in alignment with your organizational goals. See Figure 5.8 for an example using our old imaginary friend, Roadshare Chicago.

The key to measuring the impact of social media campaigns is to keep the focus on what happens after you publish on a social network. Social media exists to engage people, so your goal should be to track metrics that capture conversation, sharing and other forms of participation.

Four standard metric types for social media include:

RoadShare Chicago We create healthy communities, healthy people and healthy businesses through bike lanes		
Organizational Objectives	Drive community campaigns supporting bike lane legislation	
Social Media Campaign Goals	Collect petition signatures	
Content Hypothesis	Infographic showing the impact the petition is hoping to prevent	
Key Performance Indicators	# of signatures from visitors who clicked through the campaign	% of visitors who clicked through and signed
Targets	5,000	80%
Segments	New vs. returning signers	
	Traffic sources: Facebook, Twitter, Pinterest	

Figure 5.9 By measuring hypothesis validation, product developers can make educated decisions regarding whether to abandon their hypothesis (pivot) or stay the course (persevere).

1. Volume

Volume metrics are about quantity: how many followers? How many posts and tweets? These flat metrics are useful starting points, but by themselves don't offer enough actionable information to guide your decisions other than setting a goal for improving them.

2. Engagement

Engagement metrics are the opposite of volume: they measure the quality of actions taken as a result of a social media campaign. Social engagement metrics include:

- Number of shares across platforms.
- Number of people who have entered a contest vs. number of people who liked and/ or shared it.
- Number of people who used an event hashtag vs. number of people who talked about the event without using the event hashtag.
- Number of people taking a discrete action, like writing reviews, completing a challenge, or taking an advocacy action.

In addition, engagement metrics take sentiment into account. For example, having 600 reviews on Yelp.com could be great if most of them are positive. But what if 500 of them are two stars or less?

3. Click-Throughs

Google Adwords rates are calculated by click-throughs. Here's a simple way to measure their value: count up the click-throughs you earned through social media efforts and calculate how much money you saved by earning click-throughs instead of paying for them.

4. Conversions

Some social media monitoring software can track conversions, like tickets purchased and donations made stemming from social platforms. This is by far the simplest and most direct way to determine ROI.

Figure 5.9 is a chart of starter social media campaign KPIs to kickstart your organization's planning:

Social Media Analysis Software

While it is possible to manually track social media marketing efforts across all channels, social media analysis services can make this work much more efficient by providing a single platform to manage social accounts. A good social media service will help you manage the following tasks:

- **Managing conversations:** Flagging community questions so you can respond to every person who contacts you on social media.
- **Publishing content:** Enabling you to publish on all channels from one platform.
- **Analytics:** Tracking shares, likes, conversions, etc., and creating reports.
- **Scanning for mentions:** Tracking and reporting how other people talk about your company.

Here are a few of many options:

- Sprout Social
- Hubspot
- Ubervu

Participation	Comments per post
Sharing	Retweets/shares per post
Appreciation	Favorites/likes per post
Conversion	Action on a goal promoted in the post (i.e.: donations, buying tickets)

Figure 5.10 Common and useful social media Key Performance Indicators

Mobile Metrics Strategy

There are two key strategic questions mobile metrics can help you answer: should we build a mobile optimized site, and is our mobile optimized site working?

1. Should we Build a Mobile-Optimized Site?

Let's say you have 500,000 visitors a year to your site, and your traffic report shows that about 20,000 of them use a mobile device to view it. At first glance, those numbers suggest that there's no reason to build a mobile optimized site just to make a better experience for a fraction of your visitors. However, those numbers could be explained by a range of scenarios, including:

- Those 20,000 people are at the final conversion stage and are having a hard time completing their transaction.

- 300,000 people would use a mobile optimized site, but since you don't have one they can't.
- An additional 250,000 found your site on their mobile devices and bounced away when they realized that your site wasn't mobile optimized.

The raw visit numbers simply don't provide enough context to make a decision about whether or not building a mobile optimized site is a worthwhile investment. Conducting in-depth user research (covered in depth in Chapter 2) will give you the context you need to make a data-based decision.

2. Is Our Mobile-Optimized Site Working?

The entire purpose of having a mobile-optimized site is to make it easy for visitors to achieve goals on mobile devices. The key metric to look for is conversion rate on the mobile site, and how it compares to the website. Here are a few things to try:

- Filter funnel flow visualization charts to *only* show data from mobile users. If the funnel falloff is significantly different than that of desktop users, you might reconsider mobile.
- Likewise for goal conversions.
- Filter bounce rate by only mobile device users. This may not offer the most accurate data regarding mobile site usability because some search terms will point users to a specific blog post that a mobile user may simply not be interested in. However, if the bounce rate is *significantly* higher than that of desktop users it might be something to consider.

Benchmarking Measurement Strategy

Benchmarks show specific comparative data over time. In other words, you can track improvement (or lack thereof). Once you've chosen KPIs, track data at regular intervals so you can measure improvement. Whether this is on a daily, weekly, monthly, or quarterly basis is up to you. The important thing is to set up an environment where improvements (or drops) can be easily tracked side-by-side. If you're not using an analytics tool that provides this for you, a spreadsheet will suffice.

Here are some questions to ask when benchmarking data:

1. Is what we're doing having an effect on customer/user behavior?
2. If so, how much? (positive or adverse effect?)
3. How can we improve the positive effects of our efforts?
4. How often should we compare results?
5. How do we decide whether to discontinue certain efforts based on our data?

Once you have answered these questions, set dates for comparing benchmarks in your calendar and begin tracking the data. Notable shifts in the data over time should inform whether or not you pivot from a particular campaign effort or continue efforts to improve it.

Iteration

Remember those targets and objectives you defined in the measurement strategy chapter? How about the user task flows in the design strategy chapter? Here's where those come full-circle to help improve website performance over time. Everything on your website offers a potential hypothesis to prove or disprove. Do you think your email campaign or social media efforts are generating sales leads? Let's test that. Do your white papers and videos actually get downloaded or watched all the way to the end? Let's find out. Is your shopping cart checkout process as streamlined for users as it can possibly be? A cart analytics funnel can tell you. Using goals, funnels and other analytics tools can help you validate whether or not the hypothesis is worth pivoting from for another course, or sticking to for a longer period of time to improve upon your success.

Setting up goals in an analytics package means taking the targets you defined during strategy sessions and equating them with actions that users take on your website. For example, if your target is to reach 500 white paper downloads over the course of a month, setting up a goal in your analytics package is the first step in measuring the path to success. In this example, a goal completion would be the successful download of a white paper, which could be measured by a user reaching the 'Thank you for downloading our white paper' page on your site.

If a month passes and you're only at 150 downloads you have a few options:

- Adjust your target to make it a more realistic expectation of your target audience.
- Try different avenues for promoting the white paper.
- Assess white paper content and devise ways to increase its sharing potential, like promoting it with an infographic visualizing a key finding.

Whichever option above you decide to pursue, good measurement tactics will give you the data points to validate or invalidate any hypothesis related to web, email, or social media performance.

Iterating based on metrics

Setting KPIs and tracking goals and funnels over time will show if your website or content campaigns are performing as well as expected. If not, what do you do? Here's where iteration comes into play. You now have data to guide improvement-driven changes in marketing strategies. Analytics data will remove much of the guesswork that may have been a part of previous online marketing efforts. You can measure what matters the most to your business over time and make improvements that lead to outcomes you desire.

Many of the decisions made around analytics and measurement are at the core of your business and in most cases the best person to answer the questions all this data presents is you. That said, many organizations share a few common challenges when it comes to implementing content iteration:

1. Establishing a timeframe
2. Interpreting goal funnels
3. Interpreting social media content signals
4. Tweaking keywords for SEO
5. Revising Channel and Velocity plans

1. Establishing a Time Frame

How much time should you give published content before analyzing its performance data and making necessary changes to your approach? That depends on how actively you are promoting different types of content and whether or not your promotion efforts remain consistent over time. In other words, a promoted post (i.e., shared across social networks, on blogs, etc.) will potentially perform better than a non-promoted post. To every rule there is an exception as well. After 6 months, a high-traffic website could pick up on your content, promote it, then traffic spikes. It is up to you to decide whether that traffic spike represents something actionable that provides results and, hopefully, that you can reproduce. Hard-and-fast rules are made to be broken in content marketing and this is one area where that is especially true. Experimentation is the name of the game. In general, the more time you give published content the more apt it is to represent actionable data.

Some time-based adjustments to consider include:

- **Reviewing channels:** What channels are driving the most traffic to your site? Can you post more often to channels that drive more qualified traffic and less often to those that don't?
- **Reviewing content types:** What blog topics are most popular? What content types get shared the most?
- **Reviewing conversions:** What content types are driving your conversions? Can you devote more time to them?

It is also worth noting that measuring specific content over time is exclusive to web performance metrics. Because of the feed-based nature of content on social networks, links tend to perform well initially and drop off quickly. So measuring something you shared on Facebook, for example, is less about performance over time and more about engagement, comments, click-throughs,

That said, measuring three months after publish date will give you a starting point to figure out whether a piece of content is performing well. With the information collected over a few months you can start making actionable recommendations.

To measure the impact of your strategy, plan a full annual review to pull actionable metrics to drive efforts for the upcoming year. With a year's worth of information you can confidently make strategic decisions, including:

- **Reviewing channels:** What channels are driving the least traffic to your site? Can you drop the channel, or should you simply reduce the time you spend there? What channels are driving the most traffic to your site? Rethink your whole strategy on those channels.
- **Reviewing content types:** Based on popularity and conversions, what kinds of content can you keep, expand, and throw away?
- **Reviewing messaging:** Are your target audiences responding to your messaging? If not, it may be time to refine your messaging strategy.

2. Interpreting Goal Funnels

When it comes to assessing content strategy and marketing efforts, funnels show where in the process you defined visitors leave your site. While a certain amount of drop-off is inevitable as visitors move along the conversion path (hence the term "funnel"), big jumps in funnels may surface content issues.

To demonstrate how, let's take a look at a typical funnel for a consulting firm's website.

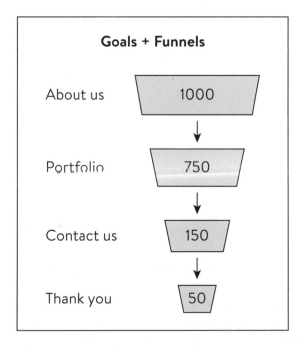

Figure 5.11

This funnel shows the number of visitors that complete each step of a conversion process in which the ultimate goal is to sign new client work. At first glance everything seems fine, but a closer looks reveals one massive drop-off: 150 people arrived at the "contact us" form but only 50 or so actually submitted it. A jump of that magnitude suggests that the "contact us" form could use some tinkering (for more detail on creating optimal forms, see Chapter 3).

Goal funnels can also help you catch breaks in your site. If, for example, no forms had been submitted that would be a good indicator that your forms are busted.

3. Interpreting social media content signals

Trends to look for in social media performance data should include engagement as well as conversion.

Engagement trends to look for:

- Patterns in the posts that get most shares.
- Patterns in the posts that get responses or start conversations.
- Patterns in posts that lead to new followers.

Conversion trends to look for:

- Patterns in posts that drive traffic to your site.
- Patterns in posts that drive conversions on your site.

Devoting time to data analysis regularly over time can help you identify trends to take action on.

4. Tweaking keywords for SEO

Keyword performance is definitely something you can measure and iterate over time. If a piece of content isn't performing well for the intended keywords and phrases, shake it up! Tweak the content, edit the metadata, add new key phrases to the body copy and see if it fares better. Be sure to track what you did, however. Benchmarking performance will help you pursue efforts that perform better and dump those that don't.

Much of this will, of course, depend on how competitive your keyword choices are. Let's be frank, all your hard work will be for naught when trying to compete for keywords others corner the market on, like iPod, for instance.

There is also a range of SEO plug-in tools you can use to speed the process, including:

- Wordpress SEO by Yoast (yoast.com)
- All in one SEO pack (http://wordpress.org/plugins/all-in-one-seo-pack/)
- Scribe SEO (scribecontent.com)

One word of caution: if any of the above plug-ins also change your URL structure, it is important to note that links from external sources will now be broken. Fix 'em or redirect the old URL to the new post.

5. Revising Channel and Velocity Plans

Both conversion and engagement data should inform your channel and velocity plans. As you publish more and more content, your analytics will show you which topics people are most interested in. In the short term it makes sense to create more content on those topics but still continue creating content according to all your strategic categories. Then, once a year or so you can take a step back and look at your category choices with an eye to cutting the low-performers, expanding the top performers, and possibly trying out some new categories as well.

Monitoring your visitors' common questions is another way to identify potential new topics. After all, visitors can't read content that isn't there. Listening for common questions directed both to your company and being discussed in your field in general is a great way to add topics to your content creation list over time. Once the content is created, you can then monitor its performance through your analytics dashboard.

Conclusion

In this chapter we provided an overview of what it takes to build an effective digital marketing measurement strategy and improve upon it over time. Here's what we discussed:

- The information web analytics software captures, including visitors, traffic sources, page views, and bounce rates.
- Four principles for planning your overall digital measurement strategy.
- A three-step process to identify your organization's Key Performance Indicators (KPIs).
- How to set up goals and funnels in your analytics software in order to track conversions.
- The information social media software can help you manage, including publishing and conversation tracking.
- The role of benchmarking in your digital strategy.
- Iterating your content strategy based on performance metrics

Profile

Figure 5.12 Rand Fishkin

Rand Fishkin

CEO & Co-founder, Moz

Rand Fishkin is the CEO & Co-founder of Moz, a Seattle-based startup focused on helping marketers track and improve inbound channels like SEO, social media, content, links, brand mentions, etc. He shared his insights on choosing performance metrics wisely.

Search continues to grow unabated—we've never had two consecutive quarters where desktop search queries fell year over year, and mobile just keeps skyrocketing. Unfortunately for SEO professionals, the overarching trend of Google's ongoing algorithm changes is to make data less transparent. For example, link data, PageRank, and social connection tools have been phased out and there are frustrating inconsistencies in the data we do still get from sources like Google Webmaster Tools.

All of this means we're less and less aware of how Google operates, how people use Google, how they use it to get to our sites, and what we can do to improve. This should violate Google's core values and beliefs around transparency, but so far, I don't see any signs of them stopping.

This makes it more important than ever to choose your performance metrics wisely. I'm actually not always against vanity metrics. In some cases, they can be useful and worthwhile. But the right metrics to track are those that map to your goals, and measure progress.

For example, if you are converting customers via the web, or attracting them online and converting them in the real world, the first thing you need is some sense of your funnel, and how people move through the various stages to convert. This can reveal where bottlenecks and opportunities might lie.

Next, I'd focus on some calculation of Customer Lifetime Value (CLTV) and Customer Acquisition Cost (CAC) along with gross margin. Those three are the lifeblood of your business, and will tell you whether, when, and how to scale.

When it comes to analyzing metrics, there's no one cut and dried single way to decide which metrics changes are significant and which are just noise. Every business and every marketer will have different results depending on their inputs and their situation (and all the potential things that might cause flux). Listing and understanding all the elements that can cause a metric to fluctuate is a valuable exercise, though.

The one critical skill you need is empathy: the ability to get into another person's head and understand how they're feeling, what they're thinking, and why. No skill will serve you further because, as marketers, we are trying to help them solve problems, answer questions, and be delighted. Metrics are a means to an end: understanding if we're succeeding.

CHAPTER SIX

Writing for the Web

The secret to creating consistently good writing is constraints. You want all your inspiration and innovation to go to creating irresistible information and entertainment, not to dithering over voice and structure.

In this chapter, we cover how to create a set of practical web writing guidelines that everyone in your organization can use to create stellar content.

Cross-Content Guidelines

Here are some guidelines that may be applied to all types of content you create: web, blog, social media, etc.

Start with Strategy

First things first: who are you writing for and what do you want them to do? Always start with a quick review of your strategy to make sure goal and target audience drive the process of content creation.

I like to borrow a page from web developers and create a user story to describe the audience, their goals, and the desired outcome for my piece before I begin writing. Then, since I'm also writing to create a desired outcome for my organization, I add another line to account for my goals. For example:

- As a content strategist at a nonprofit, I want to learn some tips for using Pinterest to collaborate with other organizations. As the writer, I want readers to sign up for our newsletter.
- As a member of the Transportation Department, I want peer-reviewed research showing the benefits to businesses of bike lanes. As the writer, I want the reader to use and cite our research.
- As a supporter of the arts, I want to donate money to a local theater that works with at-risk kids in my neighborhood. As the writer, I want them to donate to my theater.

Define Your Voice

Who exactly is writing? Is it you, the content strategist who loves bikes and crochet? Or is it your organization, sharing decades of experience and authority? Create editorial guidelines that define the appropriate voice and tone for different types of content. Clearly defined rules make it much easier for both writers and editors. Editorial guidelines can also drive keyword use for writers as well.

Here are some example rules for content creators at our Content Strategy Framework example company, Roadshare Chicago.

Blog Posts

Voice	1st person, the writer
Slang and vernacular	Use it to humanize content. Back away from foul language though.
Industry Jargon	Not unless strictly necessary.
Images	Gorgeous scenery, smiling people, action shots
Keywords	Local trails, families

White Papers

Voice	3rd person, the organization
Slang and vernacular	Inappropriate
Industry Jargon	Could be appropriate, depending on industry
Images	Charts, graphs, bustling businesses with bikes
Keywords	Business, economy

Include "best practice" content examples in your guidelines. Ideally, these will be content from your organization, but it can also be helpful to include examples from companies you like.

Industry jargon can often sound like bad '90s marketing copy so use it sparingly. People tend to relate to things written in universal, easy-to-understand terms.

Figure 6.1 Bay Area B Corp Method Cleaning Products uses a fun and informal voice to convey brand attributes

Define Content Structure

Remember when your high school English teacher taught you the good ol' five paragraph essay structure? Just write an introductory paragraph, three supporting paragraphs, and a conclusion and voila! An A grade! You can recreate that clarity for your writers by providing basic structures for different forms of content. For example:

Blog Post Structure Options

List	Tips, examples, DIY ideas
Review	Insights and impressions from an exhibit, performance, or book
How-to	Step-by-step instructions for a task
Event	Come to our party! Here's why, and here's when and where

Tweet Structure Options

Tip of the hat	Sharing a neat thing another person in the community did
Thank you	Thanking a member of the community who did something nice for you
Free gift	Alerting people to a sweet offer
Invitation	Come to our awesome event; here are the details
See you there	We are attending an awesome event and you should come too.
Promotion	Check out this cool, useful content we created

Case Study Structure Template

Similarly, you can use this six-step process to draft a case study targeted toward customer needs:

1. Introduction	Write an impact quote/story stating the benefit.
2. Before	Summarize the situation before the intervention.
3. During	Walk through the steps in the process of the intervention.
4. After	Because of our intervention, happiness reigned. This is how.
5. Result	Statistics underlying the personal impact of the intervention.
6. CTA	End with call-to-action: Call us, we can help you succeed, too.

Blogging Like a Boss

Remember that velocity plan you created in Chapter 2, which outlined your primary blog topics and post frequency for the upcoming year? Use it as the starting point for brainstorming topics and recruiting writers and editors for your blog.

Recruiting Writers

It is common practice for an organization to ask employees to blog. This can provide valuable perspectives about topics across the organization, not just the marketing department. Alas, most people aren't professional writers so the prospect of writing anything for publication can be intimidating.

Here are some ideas for making it as easy as possible to empower employees to write for the company blog:

1. **Explain why you're asking them to write.** When you're adding to a coworker's already full workload, transparency and flexibility go a long way toward making this effort successful. In our experience, it's much better to recruit writers in a face-to-face conversation or meeting rather than an email.

   Start with your Content Strategy Framework and show how blogging supports your organization's business goals. Explain that they have expertise that your customers are interested in. Assure them that you have guidelines to help them write, and that they can choose topics that interest them. Close with a reiteration of the fact that this is not busywork, you are asking them to contribute their expertise in the service of meeting the organization's goals. Then thank them. Try smiling.

2. **Create a comprehensive set of editorial guidelines.** These should include:
   - The strategy, structure and voice constraints that we covered in the beginning of this chapter.
   - Directions on how writers should source their facts and guidelines on acceptable and unacceptable sources.
   - Directions on how to source visuals for posts, including photos, infographics, and videos.

- Recommended word counts and recommended hours to spend on each post. At Mightybytes, we aim for 500 words and 4-ish hours of work per blog post.
- Formatting guidelines. For example: "Chunk content into short paragraphs and/ or use lists or bullets for ease of reading."
- Handy writing tools. For example, we like the Flesch-Kinkaid readability level tool, a quick and easy way to check that your writing is easy to read for your target audience. As an added bonus, it comes installed in MS Word.
- Keyword lists and how to use them.

3. **Teach the basics of Search Engine Optimization.** Your writers should understand SEO basics. They're writing first for people, not machines, but understanding concepts like keywords and metadata can make your content read well for people *and* taste great to search engines.

Anoint an Editor

In addition to a smart strategy and good writing, nearly all web content requires some sort of editorial work as well. Whether that entails swapping out key phrases or tweaking copy tone, spelling, grammar and clarity, few posts are successful without undergoing some sort of rigorous quality assurance process before hitting the "Publish" button. Make sure you have an editorial gatekeeper who can serve this role.

Email Like an Emperor

Marketing emails are carefully orchestrated pieces of content that add value to readers and inspire further exploration of a topic, hopefully inciting a click-through to a more detailed explanation that lives on your website and is easily sharable. Respect your readers and, as with any other type of content, give them something worthy of their time. Your email pours into their inbox alongside everyone else's. The best way to ensure it isn't fated for the trash bin is to make the content as compelling and easily digestible as possible.

When properly executed, email campaigns are a tried and true, cost-effective marketing tactic. In fact, as of 2011 the average ROI for email marketing was $44.25 for every dollar spent.[1] Put some strategic thought into your approach and see impressive jumps in your returns.

Blast-Free Zone

Don't send "email blasts." Don't do it. In fact, wipe the term from your vocabulary. Send brief, smartly constructed story teasers that add value and contain clear, concise calls-to-action. Despite popular misconceptions, your email newsletter is not the place for that lengthy tome you wrote on the company's new product or service. A sentence or two may be appropriate, and even that should be focused on benefit/ value to customers rather than how awesome you think it is. Branded emails are not the place for all 2,000 words of that "thought leadership" piece you penned when you couldn't sleep the other night either. Few customers want to open an email from you and read about a recent company paintball excursion. They just don't. Yet people use the vehicle of email marketing for these purposes all the time and, rather than drawing customers in, you're just annoying them.

Value propositions are a recurring theme in this book and so we'll say it again: create content that adds value to those who read it. Be useful and promote two-way dialogue whenever possible. You shouldn't *blast* your customers with anything except maybe a water gun and that's only if they're at your company picnic (or after the aforementioned paintball excursion). Seriously, it's disrespectful to readers and the snippet of time you're hoping to earn from them.

You spent all that time conducting comprehensive research on what customers want—give it to them. Don't water down the content's value with repeated sales pitches or marketing buzzwords. Instead, use the pointers in the upcoming two sections to keep your readers reading . . . and clicking.

Email Content Planning

As always, start with your Content Strategy Framework and identify goals, audience, conversion, and performance metrics for the email campaign. Then, write up your user story so you can keep your audience and your goals front and center as you create.

In this section, we cover special considerations for creating great email marketing content that include planning for mobile, segmenting your audience, identifying email triggering events, offering opt-in velocity plans, and limiting your content to one message and one call to action.

Make it Mobile

Remember that Mobile First strategy we talked about in Chapter 4? Make sure that your email content reads well and looks good on mobile devices. Create content that is optimized first for mobile devices and then other platforms. Here are a few eye-opening statistics on email marketing and mobile:

- 79% of smartphone owners use them for reading email, a higher percentage than those who use them for making calls.[2]
- More email is read on mobile devices than on desktop email clients.
- 45% of holiday season emails are opened on mobile devices.
- Mobile purchasing decisions are most influenced by emails from companies (71%) and only surpassed by the influence of friends (87%).[3]

Create campaigns that support a Mobile First approach by keeping content short and to-the-point and resizing images or graphics to improve load speed time. And, of course, links embedded in emails on a mobile device should lead to the campaign landing page. If the mobile "sniffer" on your website overrides an email link and dumps users out at a default mobile homepage, you've lost them.

If email marketing is core to your strategy, it may be worthwhile to invest in a service that enables you to test how your email campaigns look across multiple email clients and devices. That way you can catch any bugs before you reach out to your list. Services to check out include:

- litmus.com
- previewmyemail.com
- Emailonacid.com

Audience Segmentation

The splendid thing about email marketing is that you can customize your messages to your target audiences in a way that you simply can't on your website. Everyone who reaches your site sees the same content, so you have to write for the broadest possible audience. Email marketing lets you divide your email list by target audience and then customize the tone, content, and calls-to-action.

After all, the more relevant an email's content is to the recipient the more likely they are to open it and take sweet, delicious action. An audience segment is a group of

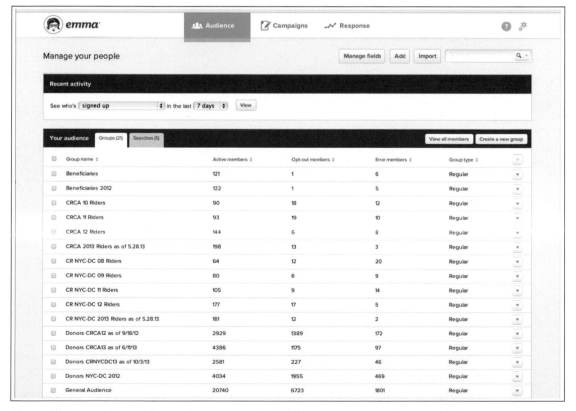

Figure 6.2 Most email marketing software will let you create groups from users who have clicked-through to a specific story. This is a sample of audience segments used in Climate Ride's email marketing campaigns.

people with shared interests or attributes. Your audience segments should correspond to the target audiences you identified during strategy sessions.

Creating Great Email Content

Sharing information in a one-way medium is only seeing half the picture. An email campaign's biggest strengths (and goals) lie in users clicking through to get more information on a particular subject. If you elicit a response of some sort, then your readers are likely engaged and your success ratio will increase.

Good email marketing either persuades the reader to take an action that benefits both them and your organization or deepens your relationship with them. The key is to limit each email to just one message and just one call to action. Examples include:

Calls to Action

- "Read more" (ie: driving qualified traffic to site content)
- RSVP to an event
- Purchase a product
- Donate

Relationship Deepening messages

- Thank you
- Reporting program or volunteer campaign success
- Free gift
- Holiday message

Whittling your message down this way can pose a challenge to organizations accustomed to sending out wordy newsletters with lengthy stories, but studies show that focused messages lead to more conversions.[4]

Links and Calls-to-Action

Writing calls-to-action that drive successful click-through rates is a black art. Matching customer personas to content needs during strategy sessions should give you a conceptual foundation to build upon, but figuring out exactly what words on the button prompt action takes a fair bit of trial and error.

Here are some things to note when trying to incite a specific action:

- You are giving your reader instructions. Don't shy away from action-oriented verbs like *buy, subscribe,* and *share.*
- Clearly state the result of the action. Examples include *Vote for our sustainability panel* or *Buy your own hot pants in our store.*
- Frame the action in terms of benefit to the reader. Examples include *Get your free trial now* and *Find a gorgeous trail near you.*

Figure 6.3 Calls to action don't get much clearer than "Create free photo product."

We will talk more about measuring email campaign performance in later chapters, but remember that many email marketing platforms use the anchor text of a hyperlink when generating click-through performance reports. If you only use "click here" or "read more" for calls-to-action in your campaign, then your report will be filled with nothing but "click here" or "read more," making it hard to decipher which links had high click-through rates and which didn't.

Descriptive Subject Lines

According to MailChimp's email subject line research,[5] using your customer's name in the subject line doesn't increase open rates, but using their city name does. Thirty-three percent of recipients open an email based on subject line alone. It's the first thing that people see, so make the subject line a strong one. Your goal is to write a subject line that—wait for it—describes the content of the email. You did all that work to create content to appeal to the specific audience you are targeting, so trust it. Direct, factual statements will get more attention than gimmicks or pushy sales language.

Here are a few subject lines from my inbox that clearly state a tangible and actionable benefit to users:

- Organize Your Social Media Accounts with Hootsuite
- New Chicago Meetup: Drinks for Working Parents
- Summer Soccer League Registration Now Open
- Last Day: Free Shipping on Toys

For fun, here's a selection of terrible subject lines I found in my inbox:

- 29 Days to Be Thankful
- In the Spirit of Holiday Giving
- This Company Could Rally Cause of Low Float

These subject lines are vague and/or incomprehensible, and are destined for the Recycle Bin if I ever bother to clean out my inbox.

Body Content: KISS

Keep it short and sassy (or salacious or simple or any other adjective starting with "s" that you prefer). Yes, it is challenging to whittle your information down to a single key message with corresponding call-to-action. In fact, you might spend more time editing than writing to make this happen, but it will be worth the effort.

Keep your writing style terse, professional, and benefits-driven, but also unique in a manner that reflects you or your organization's personality. Now is not the time for flowery prose but rather to showcase your professionalism and ability to communicate key topics in as little space as possible. No matter what your message is, the following principles will help you frame your content most appealingly:

- Write to a single person: the bystander effect will prevail (i.e., "someone else will do it") if you address your email to a group. Customize to a specific person whenever possible.
- Establish the relevance of your message. If your readers are getting the email because they are senior executives, mention that up top.
- Use headers: if your email campaign has more than one story, use headers and maybe short subheads to draw their attention to the most important topics.
- Each "story" in your email should be two or three sentences with a link that leads somewhere else (preferably your website). This keeps the body content short and gets potential customers to your site.
- Keep stories to a minimum: just because you have mastered the fine art of the 2–3 line story teaser doesn't mean you should include a dozen of them. That diffuses your message and creates distractions.
- Include easy to find calls-to-action. Make them clearly clickable.
- Use active verb tense (do this vs. had done this) when possible. It is more immediate.
- Overall, keep word count to a bare minimum.

Write for Designers

No, I'm not talking about your subject matter. I'm talking about making sure the intent of your content is clear to those who will turn your beautiful prose into even more beautiful designs. Establishing copy mark-up conventions that writers and designers both follow will make collaboration a much simpler affair.

These shared mark-up conventions should cover:

1. **Visual hierarchy.** Good design uses visual hierarchy to guarantee that your most important information will be seen first. Writers should mark up their copy so that designers know exactly what the most important information is.
2. **Links.** Writers should always include the destination links the content leads to.
3. **Images.** Any supporting image needs should be clearly marked so designers know what to create.
4. **Calls-to-action.** These should be clearly labeled as such so the design's visual hierarchy can represent their importance accordingly.

H1: This headline rules

H2: This is the most interesting body copy I have ever read for the following reasons:

- It's short
- It's to the point
- It reminds me of Nicholas Cage winking (link to: http://replygif.net/1119)

This headline rules

This is the most interesting body copy I have ever read for the following reasons:

➢ It's short
➢ It's to the point
➢ It reminds me of Nicholas Cage winking

Figure 6.4 Mark-up conventions are a simple way to help content creators and designers collaborate effectively.

Designing Email Templates

Email marketing software almost always offers a host of pre-built templates to choose from. But if you want to maintain consistent brand identity, consider spending the time up front to create a custom HTML email marketing template that effectively represents your existing visual identity. Also, oftentimes it is not enough to merely design a good email template that employs your logo. Design integrity should be maintained across the entire click-path, including auto-responders, campaign forms, sign-up screens, preferences, landing pages, and other campaign elements. A consistent and recognizably branded look will help assure best performance.

Maintaining design integrity in an email campaign can be one of the biggest challenges in its execution and a source of frustration for designers. Email campaign tools vary greatly in features offered and email clients like Outlook, Gmail, and Apple Mail support different implementations of campaign content, which means what looks beautiful in one client is completely messed up in another.

If you've ever opened up an email from a company you've done business with and been confronted with walls of text, weird colors and broken links, you know just how important design is to email marketing. Here are some things to consider when you're designing custom email marketing templates.

Create Campaigns to Match Your Brand[6]

Sounds simple, right? You would be surprised at how many companies don't design campaigns that are in line with their brand standards. Consistent, brand-friendly design provides instant connection and recognition for readers. If users can identify with a familiar brand or campaign, their experience is more personal and they're more likely to engage with the campaign's content. If not, you lost them on first glance.

Kelly McClain, a graphic designer for an email marketing service called Emma, writes precisely on this topic in Five Pointers for Visually Effective Email Campaigns on the Emma blog. Kelly's post discusses how successful imagery, design elements and typography are used in the Oprah Newsletter she gets each Monday, saying ". . . what keeps me hooked is that whenever I open it, I know exactly where to direct my eyes for a hasty once-over . . . I start clicking the links that appeal to me [because] the email stays consistent within itself, using only a couple of fonts (in reasonable sizes) and sticking to a uniform, easy-to-read color scheme."

Fonts Matter

Pay special attention to font use when designing a campaign. Keep type simple and legible. Don't waste your readers' time by making them figure out the visual hierarchy of your campaign on their own. Give them solid typographical structures that support easy scanning to identify headlines, links, and so on. And, of course short, bulleted lists are always easy on the eyes.

Use web-safe fonts ONLY for text-based content in your email marketing. Why? In short, emails are meant to be much simpler than web content and many advanced CSS (or JavaScript) tricks won't work. Web-safe fonts include just the basics: Arial, Times, Georgia, Tahoma, etc.

Of course with Photoshop, Illustrator, or a slew of other image editing tools, it's a simple process to export type as an image, but use this sparingly. Not everyone will be able or willing to view images in their email, particularly if they're reading it on an older mobile phone. Plus, if your email is also archived on your own site (which it should be), the keyword-rich text copy will be picked up by search engines as well, bolstering your search engine credibility.

Use Images Sparingly

Oversized images or broken image links can be a straight shot to the "unsubscribe" button. Exporting images for email campaigns is a delicate balancing act between small file size and image quality. Optimize images enough to ensure speedy download on even the slowest connections but make sure that they still look good. Yahoo's SmushIt tool is free and works really well for optimizing images if you don't happen to have an image editing tool like Photoshop.

Don't Use Animation and Rich Media

Rich media offers the opportunity for higher levels of campaign engagement, but the number of hurdles to successful implementation far outweighs the benefits. It's easier just to include a linked player image to this content on your own site than to embed Flash or video files that may not be supported by your customers' email accounts.

Use Vertical, Not Horizontal Scrolling

If scrolling through your content offers a better user experience, then go for it. Cramming content into a tight, constrained layout doesn't make any sense in a media format where users are already used to the idea of scrolling. Sure, it's probably a good idea to put your most important piece of news towards the top to increase views and potential click-throughs, but remember that users will naturally scroll a page if the content is longer than their screen. This is especially true if the page they're viewing is designed to be used that way, as with email campaigns. Keep your campaign width optimized for lowest common denominators since not all scrolling is created equal. Your template should be 600 pixels wide or less.

Create Absolute Paths

Many campaign software packages won't support hosting embedded images or relative paths, so be sure to include a complete absolute path to any embedded content. In other words, all links and images in your email should point to the same location on the same system.

Delivering Great Email Content

Campaign Velocity Plans

Campaign velocity plans specify how many individual emails will be delivered, how they will be staggered, and where the call-to-action link should take readers.

When you mapped out your content strategy, you created an overall email marketing velocity plan establishing how frequently you plan to email your lists. That decision about email frequency should inform the velocity plan for each individual email campaign. This helps you keep the big picture in mind: even if you do provide value to readers, sending too often can be the quickest way to the unsubscribe button for many busy folks on your list.

One trick that big companies with vast subscriber lists (think Amazon, Kraft, and Target) use is to give their email subscribers a choice when it comes to email frequency. For example, subscribers could choose daily deals, weekly recipe collections, or monthly coupons. This approach is best for companies that have big enough subscriber lists that the return on investing the time in creating tiers of subscriber content is worthwhile; most smaller organizations shouldn't bother.

Drip Marketing

Drip marketing messages are triggered by specific events, rather than by audience segments. For example, if a potential customer has put a bunch of items in the shopping cart on your website but hasn't checked out, that would be an event that triggers an email message reminding them to complete their purchase.

The purpose of creating a drip marketing plan is to make your marketing team's life easier by automating emails that you can predict and plan for rather than responding to them on a one-on-one basis.

Types of drip marketing campaign triggering events include:

- Membership is expiring in one month, triggering a reminder to renew.
- A free trial request, triggering a welcome and sign-in message.
- Monetary donation, triggering a "thank you." For nonprofits, people who have just completed a donation should get a series of "welcome" messages that build up the relationship with thank yous and success stories before they get another "donation" message.
- A white paper is downloaded, triggering a thank you, and "was this helpful, please take our survey" message.

Spam, Spam, Spam, Spam, Spammity-Spam, Horrible Spam

The CAN-Spam Act of 2003 set some ground rules for what marketers who want to use email as a marketing tool can and cannot do:

- Sender must provide clear details for users to opt-out.
- Sender must honor opt-out requests promptly.
- Sender must include their physical address.
- Sender must not use false or misleading subject lines.
- Sender must not use deceptive subject lines.
- If an email is an ad it must be described as such.
- Sender must monitor what others are doing on their behalf (i.e. email marketing services, vendors, etc.).[8]

Your drip marketing plan should be built based on the visitor actions you identified in your strategy plan and data you've collected from your analytics system or from user research on common obstacles and other events that require follow-up.

Delivery Time Counts

Be mindful of when you send out emails. In their infographic, aptly titled *The Best Time to Send Email*,[7] the folks at GetResponse analyzed 21 million messages sent from their system to determine the best open and click-through rates on campaigns. Their findings: 8:00 to 10:00 in the morning and 3:00 to 4:00 in the afternoon can increase click-through rates by up to 6%.

Of course, there are many other factors at play with click-through rates, and you should look to your own knowledge about your subscribers. For example, if you have customers in multiple time zones that's more relevant to your delivery time plans than one, admittedly cool, study.

Testing: The Secret to Creating Killer Content

Following the guidelines outlined in this section is a good start, but then comes the fun part: testing! A/B testing subject lines is the easiest way to begin. Simply write two different subject lines for the same email, then send the A subject line to 10% of your mailing list and the B subject line to another 10%. Whichever one provides the best open rate gets sent to the remaining 80% of your list!

Again, if you send content of value to your users none of the above should be much of a problem. Email marketing software platforms are required by law to adhere to the above, and the majority have built-in features for opt-outs, footer templates that include contact information, and so on. They monitor the content sent out on their systems and if something doesn't adhere to the points above the sender is immediately notified.

There are a multitude of resources to help you test the success of your email campaigns, and taking the time to use them will reap big rewards. But don't take our word for it: check out Dan Siroker and Pete Koomen's book, *A/B Testing*. They honed their approach in the 2008 Obama campaign and the book is a series of killer case studies—with pictures!

Conclusion

In this chapter, we outlined practical tips for creating killer content, including:

- Basic guidelines for writing for the web.
- Creating valuable content for your blog and recruiting company writers.
- How to write effective email marketing content, including audience targeting and testing.

Figure 6.5 Jill Pollack

Profile

Jill Pollack
Founder and Director, StoryStudio Chicago and Words for Work

StoryStudio Chicago teaches people how to tell their stories. In their creative writing programs, they help students from all walks of life find the stories they want to tell. Then, they teach them the craft to tell those stories using their unique voices. Their business writing students learn both storytelling techniques and communications strategies, as well as the value that good communication brings to almost any situation. Their students gain the confidence to believe that their stories matter.

Jill Pollack is the founder and director of StoryStudio Chicago. She is the founder of the Chicago Literary Alliance and is an author, teacher, and a presenter who talks about the power of telling our story in our personal and professional lives. Jill has created interactive training programs for many Fortune 1000 clients including Motorola, McDonald's Corporation, Lands' End, Sears Roebuck and Co., Equity Office Properties, DePaul University, and the University of Illinois at Chicago. Jill has published three books for young adults: *Shirley Chisholm*; *Lesbian and Gay Families: Redefining Parenting in America,* and *Women on the Hill*, a history of women in Congress and has written for a wide variety of newspapers and magazines.

What is the primary goal of StoryStudio's content and digital marketing efforts?

Our primary goal with our digital marketing is to simply inform our audiences what opportunities we have for them. We don't use any traditional media for that. No more print advertising or even PR stories. For us, it's all about engaging with those students and Friends of StoryStudio who have indicated that they want to be in the know. We do however also use our digital media to continue the education process and to keep the conversation going.

What is your biggest marketing challenge?

Right now lack of staff is our biggest challenge. There is so much more we can be doing— both in the digital and in the real world—to connect with our audiences. We've had to be incredibly choosy about where to put our energy since we operate with such a small staff.

What role does storytelling play in content marketing?

For StoryStudio, and for anyone who employs content marketing, storytelling is key. It's how humans have always learned and how they have always built community. Good stories come from having an authentic voice and the sincerity to build trust.

If you were to impart one critical idea to a would-be content marketer about telling stories on the web, what would it be?

It's hard to pick one, of course. I always tell students that writing is not one-way communication; good writing invites the reader to get involved in this dialogue and I believe that's what good Content Marketing is too.

How do you blend the art of storytelling with the often technical practice of targeting keywords, optimizing pages for search engines, and so on?

Ah, that's kind of an age-old issue for writers. We are always having to balance the art and science of communications and finding the right SEO mix is no different.

I may be unpopular for saying this, but I will always sacrifice SEO if it means not doing so will produce a bad story poorly told. Having said that, I would also say that if the key words and such don't seem to fit, you better have another plan to make sure your content is being found.

What advice would you give to content creators wanting to move beyond the blog post?

Instead of thinking just beyond the blog, I encourage content marketers to think holistically. What are all the tools—in person, print, and digital—that you can employ and how will they interact with each other. We are often asked to train teams on how to tell a story across multiple platforms and I love being in that space. Because if you are clear on the story you want to tell, then it can be great fun using the various elements and opportunities different media present.

How do you promote your content and programs?

At StoryStudio we tend to focus on the places we are certain our audiences are looking. This includes Twitter and Facebook. But over the years, we've built up a loyal email newsletter list, and this is where we share our big news. We've decided not to use many other great social media tools because I think it's hard to be everywhere and do a good job everywhere. We tend to make hard choices and then concentrate our efforts.

StoryStudio has done a great job at building community in the brick and mortar world. How do you extend that idea to your virtual properties, like your blog, website, and social networks?

This is an interesting question and one that we've pondering for a long time. The chemistry of the classroom really produces magic and there's no exact equivalent of that in the online world.

But we do provide individual online space to our classes so students can continue to connect in between class sessions. We'll also be launching our version of online classes this fall. I say "our version" because instead of trying to replicate the traditional classroom—which I really don't think works well online—we are using online portals as a component in our learning experiences. We're really excited about these hybrid opportunities and are partnering with a local startup that has built a community platform that includes file sharing, chat, and video.

Our corporate training clients are already taking advantage of online tools and we now do quite a bit of training for companies that combines in-person classroom sessions with online follow up and coaching sessions.

How do you measure success in your content marketing efforts? How do you improve upon that success?

While analytics can teach us about how effectively we're reaching our audiences, the biggest marker for us is really student enrollment. I'm pleased to say that we're trending

20–25% higher enrollment this year over last, and I do attribute much of that to a focus on our social media engagement.

What is your loftiest content marketing goal for the next year or two?

My loftiest content marketing goal is to have a staff person be responsible for providing useful information about storytelling and writing to our business and creative writing students. What I mean is, that staff person would only be responsible for this type of content, not doing a hundred things like we are all doing now.

Is there any other advice that you'd like to share with others?

My best advice is that whatever you are writing or sharing with your audience, take your time with it. Read it at least three times. Consider the message. Have someone act as your editor to proofread and challenge your assumptions. And then, after all that, read what you have written and ask yourself if you have reached high enough and have you asked your audience to dream big enough. The biggest mistake content marketers can make is to underestimate their audiences.

Notes

1. Direct Marketing Association, "Power of Direct," 2011, www.the-dma.org/cgi/dispannounce ments?article=1590
2. Adobe, "2013 Digital Publishing Report: Retail Apps & Buying Habits," 2013, www.emailmonday. com/mobile-email-usage-statistics
3. Adobe, "2013 Digital Publishing Report: Retail Apps & Buying Habits," 2013, www.emailmonday. com/mobile-email-usage-statistics
4. Mailchimp, "Effects of List Segmentation on Email Marketing Stats," http://mailchimp.com/ resources/research/effects-of-list-segmentation-on-email-marketing-stats/#section_segment_ by_interest_groups
5. Mailchimp, "How Do I Know If I'm Writing a Good Subject Line?", http://kb.mailchimp.com/ article/how-do-i-know-if-im-writing-a-good-subject-line
6. Kate Eyler-Werve, Mightybytes, "How to Create a Content Strategy for Library Websites," September 16, 2013, www.mightybytes.com/blog/entry/seven_design_coding_tips_for_better_ html_email_campaigns/
7. Hanna Andrzejewska, "Best Time to Send Email," http://blog.getresponse.com/best-time-to-send-email-infographic.html
8. Bureau of Comsumer Protection, "CAN-SPAM Act: A Compliance Guide for Business," September 2009, http://business.ftc.gov/documents/bus61-can-spam-act-compliance-guide-business

CHAPTER SEVEN

Producing Web Video

The folks at New Era Colorado in Boulder had a problem. Though their community had voted to migrate to local power with the explicit intent of eventually becoming 100% renewable. The massive coal-powered utility company in the area, which currently monopolized the local power system, had no plans of letting them win so easily. A well-funded smear campaign outspent New Era Colorado's efforts 2-to-1 and threatened to overturn what had already been voted on.

So New Era Colorado started a campaign at crowdsourcing site Indiegogo with the hopes of raising $20,000 to help spread the word about their efforts. The organization produced a 6-minute video to persuade potential donors. Things were moving along slowly until the post appeared on Upworthy, a news aggregation site that started in early 2012.

By the time their Indiegogo campaign was over, the folks at New Era Colorado had raised an impressive $193,018.00.

New Era's success isn't a fluke. Consider these web video statistics:

- 89 million Americans will watch 1.2 billion online videos today![1]
- 51.9% of marketing professionals worldwide named video the type of content with the best ROI.[2]
- Online video accounts for 50% of all mobile traffic.[3]

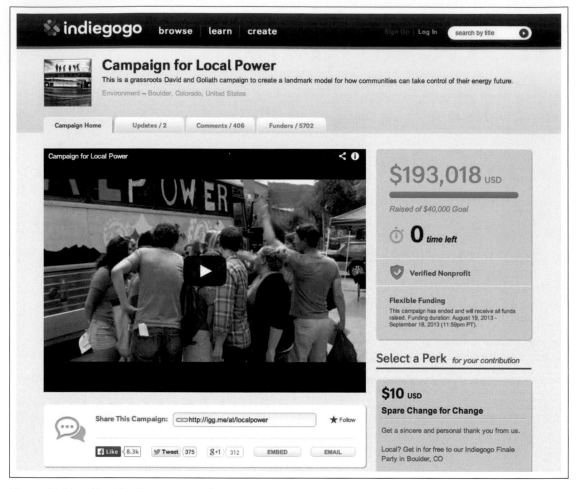

Figure 7.1 New Era's final Indiegogo tally.

Does Video Serve Your Strategy?

These numbers and New Era's story are impressive, but they don't answer the only real question: *will a web video help your organization meet its strategic goals?*

Yes, video is engaging and immediate. It is easily sharable. It works well on mobile devices. But it is also more time consuming (and subsequently costly) to create. It requires specialized skills. It uses a lot of bandwidth. It is difficult for search engines to crawl so you need to think differently about keyword use in your descriptions and other metadata. And it can be difficult to do well in a way that is so engaging that it inspires people to share it.

As ever, start by busting out your Content Strategy Framework and revisiting site goals and overall content strategy. We've created a handy-dandy decision tree to help guide your decision.

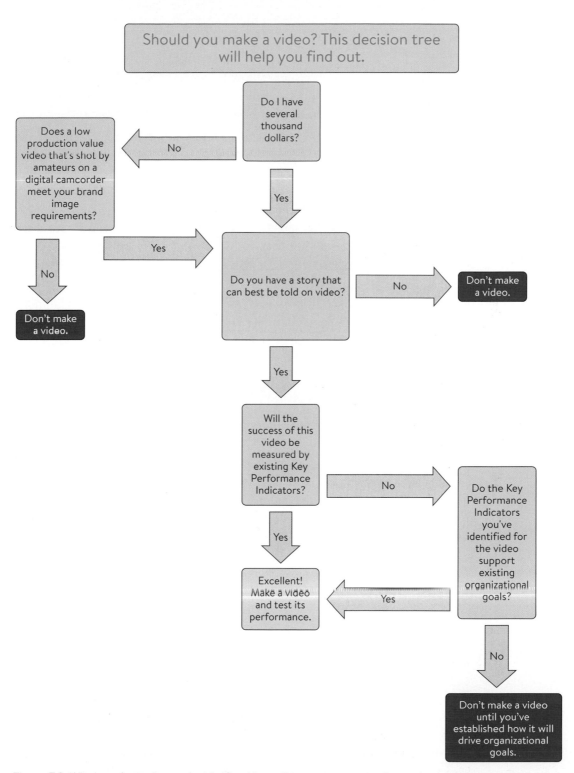

Figure 7.2 When you're trying to decide if a video will serve your strategic needs, the first question you should ask is "do I have the budget to do this right?"

Professional vs. Amateur Video Production

Matching medium to message is an important strategic decision. This is especially critical with hand-held smartphone video versus professional video production. Sometimes a shaky, handheld video shot from your co-worker's phone is the perfect option. But if you are trying to position your organization as professional, trustworthy, helpful, etc., it is worth the effort to invest in some professional quality video.

That said, big budget video projects typically guarantee high-quality production values, but as we have discussed previously, it's the *story* that's the important part. If the story you tell isn't engaging, the performance results you get from an online video will most likely fall short of your goals, no matter how much cash you throw at the video project. As much as professional video producers hate to hear this, sometimes the simple act of capturing a magical moment on your iPhone can be just as effective . . . as long as the story is good.

On the flip side, just like not everyone can be a graphic designer (though many Photoshop owners may try), the same goes for being a good video producer. Having HD video on your smartphone doesn't make you Scorsese. Know your strengths and weaknesses. Sometimes it makes a lot more sense to hire a professional video team.

To match medium to message, here are some suggestions:

- If you are capturing short, quick interviews (1–2 minutes or less), smartphone video is probably fine.
- Likewise for stupid human tricks, cat videos, and anything on Vine.
- If you need to highlight abstract concepts or showcase the inner workings of, say, a printer or car, consider hiring an animator or at the very least an illustrator.
- If your video project will be broadcast or projected anywhere beyond mobile devices or embedded into a web page, consider a professional HD video production team.
- If good lighting, steady camera work, teleprompters, greenscreens, or any other hallmarks of professionally-produced video are requirements for your project, hire a team.

If an amateur video will meet your needs, read on!

Types of Video

There are three primary categories that most online video falls into:

1. **Viral video** is aimed at driving web traffic through social sharing. Successful viral videos gain widespread viewership primarily through posting on mass video

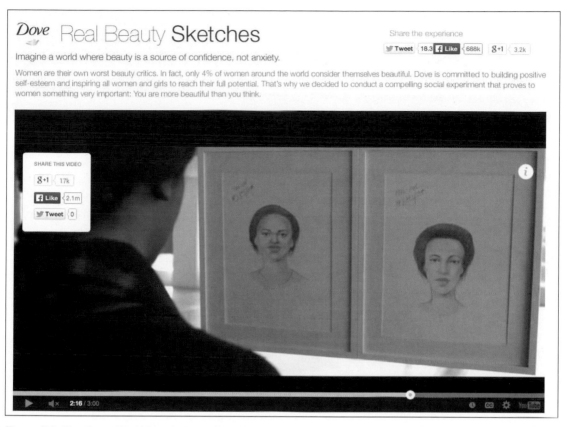

Figure 7.3 This Dove "Real Beauty" video inspired hundreds of news articles, opinion pieces, and blog posts as well as millions of likes and shares.

distribution channels such as YouTube, then become quickly and virally shared via email, posts on Facebook, Twitter and other social networks, blogs like Upworthy, Gawker, and so on. Of course, it's notoriously difficult to create a viral video. Staking your video strategy on piquing the fickle enthusiasm of a crowd can be risky business.

2. **Conversion video** is used to reach a specific goal via a call-to-action. Successful conversion videos often include professionally created content or broadcast-quality commercials that are distributed on a company or organization's website, shared via YouTube or other social sites that support video content, or forwarded via email or other "viral" channels. Not-for-profit spots or political campaign clips perform well in this arena.

Figure 7.4 Dollar Shave Club managed to create a conversion video that went viral—no mean feat.

3. **Educational video** is aimed at teaching a topic or guiding users through a process. Learning through video is plentiful on the internet now in both paid and free content channels. Online learning courses from schools and universities, video webinars, professional development, educational publisher content, and learning activities and games for children offer video content in exciting, engaging ways. Open source learning management systems like Moodle and sites like SlideShare, Udemy, eHow, and their ilk have merged educational video with course management, putting video-based online curriculum into the browsers of more people than ever.

Figure 7.5. Scrivener's videos exist to teach their customers how to use their product, rather than to pique the interest of potential customers.

These three types of video have one thing in common: they are all designed to engage people by providing content worth watching. Your visitors have endless entertainment and educational options online, so they aren't going to sit through bland marketing pitches and pushy sales ads, much less share them.

If new video isn't an option, perhaps you can capitalize on existing assets. Review current videos for relevance to content goals. A keynote by your CEO or Executive Director? Perhaps. A 2-hour video of your last board meeting? Probably not. Repurposing existing video to convey short, sharp, and memorable messages is generally cheaper and easier than starting from scratch.

Video Production Basics

It's difficult to cover everything there is to know about writing, producing, and editing your own web videos within the space of a single chapter. Instead of attempting to create a comprehensive how-to, we've assembled a number of workflow techniques necessary to maintain quality and consistency in video content. If, after reading this list of techniques, you still plan to create your own video we strongly recommend searching for additional resources and support online and in your community to help you on your way.

Video Workflow

Every video project is different and each requires a unique approach to figuring out the best way to convey a message. It's true, sometimes the best web videos come from the simple act of pointing and shooting, coupled with incredible timing. Just ask the folks who shot some of the first images of the Miracle on the Hudson or the Tahrir Square demonstrations. Since we're talking about digital marketing and not citizen journalism, we'll assume that you have chosen a planned approach over spontaneity and actually want to maintain some level of quality control over message and content throughout production.

A typical video workflow consists of some variation on the following steps:

- Budget
- Plan
- Write
- Storyboard
- Shoot
- Capture
- Edit
- Finish
- Compress

Let's get started by breaking these steps down in a bit more detail.

Budget

You are producing your video to meet an organizational goal, and your budget is your most important constraint. That means you start with your budget and figure out what's possible rather than imaging the perfect video and then try to squeeze it all in. As we covered in our decision tree at the beginning of the chapter, if you don't have the budget to make a video that meets your brand guidelines then your best bet is to create another type of content.

Plan

Good, detailed up-front planning can make a huge difference in your efforts to stay within budget and timeline parameters. Even if you're approaching your video guerilla-style on a shoestring budget with low-end tools and a production team of one or two people, your project will benefit from as much up-front leg work in the planning department as you can give it. Keep in mind that no matter how detailed you are in up-front planning, most likely the scope, timeline, and budget of the project will change, perhaps even several times, before you get a solid understanding of what it will actually take to produce. Often it is helpful to double or perhaps even triple initial estimates to get a realistic idea what a video project will cost or how much time it will take.

In the planning phase you should figure out the answers to the following questions:

- **Team:** What human resources will be needed to accomplish the production? What about a camera person, lighting expert, or director? Will you outsource it or do you have the resources to cover it internally?
- **Schedule:** How long do we need to produce this video from planning to production? Do your actors, other hires, and locations have your potential shoot dates free? Create a timeline for the entire production with the understanding that you will likely need to change it to meet ever-fluctuating expectations.
- **Casting:** Do you need actors or voice-over talent? Or do you need to find volunteers willing to go on camera to talk about how your product/service impacted their lives?
- **Production:** Outline all potential details for a shoot. How many cameras? High definition or standard definition? What's the shoot location? How much equipment and what kind? What will rentals cost?
- **Post-production:** How long will it take to edit and finish the video? How many reviews will you require? Will you need animation, graphics, or original music?
- **Output:** How many target machines or devices will your video need to play on? Is it going on a DVD? Should it play on iPhones? What sites on the web will you post it to? How much time will you need for compression and distribution?

Writing/Storyboards

Script development for web video should be focused, short, and simple, like the video itself. It also makes sense to follow your site's keyword strategy as well, since you can put transcript information into posted video's description field and metadata. Remember to keep your shots numbered in the script as well. This will help keep things organized during post-production.

- **Brainstorming:** Give yourself (and, if applicable, your team) plenty of time and creative energy to brainstorm as many creative ideas as possible. Write all ideas down. Leave nothing out.
- **Concept Development:** Whittle all your ideas down to the best two or three and flesh those concepts out further. Review with others.
- **Treatment:** The treatment is a detailed write-up of each scene in the video and its purpose is to capture the overall vision of the piece. It includes details on all aspects of

the video, including the visual style, the emotional tone, the type of music that should be playing, the desired locations, and the people/projects that will be highlighted.

- **Storyboards:** Storyboards are essentially sketches of the treatment. Even simple storyboard sketches are helpful asset to help multiple parties share the same vision.
- **Scripting:** Write the script in a language and style that is believable, speaks to the lowest common denominator of your target users (without insulting others), and sounds natural coming from your onscreen talent. And, of course, always keep the engagement factor in mind when writing. If it sounds dull and boring when you read it out loud it will sound dull and boring on screen.

Shoot

Assuming you have planned accordingly and are well-prepared on shoot day with all the appropriate equipment, cast, crew and so on, it helps to keep a few easy techniques in mind when shooting.

For best quality video in post-production, record the highest possible quality during the shoot. HD is affordable and practical these days, so consider shooting in some flavor of high definition if at all possible. This is especially critical in low-light situations. Depending on the camera, standard-definition DV tends to break apart with compression artifacts in low light. The same goes for footage that will need to be keyed. Green or blue screen footage shot in HD is much more forgiving to key than standard definition DV.

Remember the age-old rule of video production: garbage in = garbage out. If you record poor-quality footage during your shoot, all the fancy graphics and animation in the world won't make it look better. Once the footage is compressed for web output, any quality flaws will be exacerbated rather than hidden.

Also consider the following during your shoot:

- Shoot high contrast (dark background/light subject or reverse).
- Always use a tripod. Seriously.
- Avoid jerky camera movements, pans, and tilts.
- Avoid crowds and busy moving backgrounds, if possible.

For onscreen talent:

- If possible, use a teleprompter.
- Avoid bright clothing and busy patterns.
- Disable camera image sharpening settings.

To record good audio, consider the following:

- Use a lavalier or shotgun microphone. It makes a huge difference.
- Check microphone battery levels before shooting.

- Monitor audio levels with headphones at all times.
- Record 1–2 minutes of room tone/ambient presence for use in post-production.

To get the best possible image quality during the shoot, consider these suggestions:

- Use a light kit with at least two lights, preferably three: a key light, a fill light, and a back light.
- Light evenly, especially if shooting green/blue screen.
- Don't under light. Dark details can be lost in compression.
- Use a graduated neutral density filter if shooting outside.

Capture

As you film, you should file your footage based on how your script is organized to save time during editing. If you are using a tape-based workflow, this can be done as clips are captured. If you are shooting digital footage, most of this organization can be done during the shoot. Most editing software allows you to rename clips on import, create bins for clip sets, and add specific notes on each shot. Take advantage of this.

Also, backup all footage as often as necessary. If you don't have some sort of automated backup system, consider getting one. Otherwise, make regular manual backups part of your workflow. This is especially critical in a tapeless environment, as source footage cards are often erased and reused while shooting. Backing up footage to multiple drives during a tapeless shoot can save a lot of headaches (and lost footage) down the line.

Edit

If you plan to produce a lot of videos, it will help to find a set of tools that do more than you need and grow into them. Free video editing applications let you edit video without spending a dime on professional tools, but of course you get what you pay for. These editing applications are feature-limited compared to professional packages. It won't be long before you find they don't support a feature that you need to finish your video.

Your script and storyboards should serve as a solid framework for building a rough cut, a no-frills version of your video with none of the typical bells and whistles of a finished product: graphics, animation, music, sound effects, and so on. This is usually a "cuts-only" draft of the project for team review to ensure that everything is on message, on track, and no key elements or shots are missing.

Finish

Reviewing your rough cut should result in a set of tangible revisions to guide you in completing the edit. Ask for specific feedback required to create a finished video. How will titles be treated? What about lower thirds? And so on. If you don't require sign-off from a decision maker, ask for objective criticism from coworkers, friends, or even family. There are also numerous online support and user groups that offer forums with the sole purpose of getting and giving objective feedback on projects.

To ensure that you get actionable information from your critiques, use your strategic goals and KPIs to structure your test session. For example, if your video is intended to teach people how to use your product, ask people to try to use your product with only the video as a guide and see how they do. If your video is intended to persuade people to donate to your organization, ask about what surprised or moved them about the video. If at all possible, watch people's body language as they experience your video—you can pick up a lot about their levels of interest, enjoyment, boredom, and frustration that way.

At the finishing stage, you will tighten up edit points and rearrange clips as necessary to build a final cut of the video. Footage is color-corrected for consistency from beginning to end. Graphics, titles, intro animations, music and sound effects are all added and tweaked for best audiovisual impact. Upon a final review and sign-off you should have a completed video project ready to export and distribute on the web.

Compress

Video compression is the process of encoding digital video to take up less storage and transmission space. It's a trial-and-error process wherein you must find the perfect balance between audiovisual quality and playback performance. Compress a video file too little, and it could easily suffer playback hiccups, resulting in a frustrating user experience. Compress a file too much, and image quality will suffer, resulting in unreadable text, image banding, and giant blocks of dancing pixels that bear little resemblance to your original footage.

The settings used to export clips from your compressor software or video editing application are often dependent on the file types, frame sizes and resolutions supported by sites on which you plan to post the clips. Keep in mind that most video sites will re-compress your clips in order to adhere to their own set of playback standards. If you have already compressed your footage, this double-whammy can often end up in unsatisfactory results and what are known as compression artifacts, where portions of your image have degraded significantly.

This is not to say that you can't upload previously compressed video footage to YouTube or Vimeo, but if image quality is important, then you should monitor supported file specifications for the sites on which you plan to post video. Some sites won't let you post files that exceed a specific size. Others won't let you upload full-quality HD. If possible, export your video at the highest quality and maximum file size supported by the site in order to get the best possible output from the site's built-in compressors. As a general rule, as close as you can get to the original source file size, codec, and format as possible, the better quality results you will get on export.

For example, though it has improved greatly over the years, YouTube has long been known for less than adequate video quality. Exporting clips at the highest possible resolution the site supports will ensure you get the best quality once your video is live on-site.

Whichever tool you choose, try to make sure it offers variable bit-rate multi-pass encoding. The multiple encoding passes will create better looking video at smaller file sizes while the variable bit-rate will ensure smoother playback across a wider variety of machines.

While there are many occasions during the video production process where you can potentially suffer quality losses, exporting and compressing footage is by far the step during which your video can suffer the most quality degradation. Before doing a final output, run several export tests with a few seconds of footage to compare image and audio quality versus playback smoothness. If your editing software doesn't provide satisfactory results, consider using a dedicated encoding tool. Once you have found custom settings that will work best for your needs, most editing and compression software will let you save those settings so you can apply those to multiple clips down the line.

Conclusion

Producing video is an expensive, high skill, and time consuming endeavor, which makes it a high-risk content choice. After all, if a blog post doesn't get any hits you've only lost a few hours of writing and posting, but if your video doesn't get any views, shares, and conversions you've lost a big chunk of your budget.

In this chapter, we tried to talk you out of producing video unless you are very confident that it hits your overall strategy. Then, we outlined a step-by-step guide for writing and producing web video, including:

- Tying video production to your overall digital content strategy.
- Identifying your optimal video subject matter.
- Writing up a budget and then doubling it.
- Production techniques.
- Finishing and compressing video.

If you still want to produce a video, it's time to find some professionals and get cracking!

Profile

Figure 7.6 Jennifer Yee, Digital Director of B Lab.

Jennifer Yee
Digital Director of B Lab

B Lab is the nonprofit organization behind B Corporations, a global movement of entrepreneurs who are using the power of business to solve social and environmental problems. B Lab serves these entrepreneurs through certification, legislation and analytics. Companies who want to become a Certified B Corporation complete a B Impact Assessment that looks at worker engagement and benefits, community engagement, environmental impact, and governance including accountability and transparency. B Lab's initiatives provide companies with legal infrastructure and helps them attract customers, talent and capital.

Jennifer oversees digital communications for B Lab, which encompasses website management, social media, outreach and communications within the B Corporation community and with the public. She creates a lot of B Lab's content, and coordinates internal staff efforts and efforts with B Lab's marketing agency.

What is your biggest marketing challenge? How do you use content to address that challenge?

A challenge that we face is clarity and complexity. Since there are so many moving parts to the B Movement, including Certified B Corporations, benefit corporation legislation and B Analytics, we put a lot of care into clarifying each initiative and optimizing the effectiveness of each. We have created a collection of infographics and visuals to help simplify many complex ideas.

How do you capitalize on the stories of individual B Corporations within your content marketing efforts?

We recently launched a national print campaign called "Behind the Label" which tells the stories behind national brands, such as how they treat their workers, their impact on their communities, and their environmental efforts.

If you were to impart one critical idea to a would-be content marketer about the correlation between storytelling and mission-driven businesses what would it be?

Kindness is everything. Be good to every person you meet along the way and take the time to appreciate each of their stories. Mission-driven businesses will always have incredible stories to tell, but if you don't take the time to care about them—your content will fall flat. When you become truly passionate about their stories, it shows through in your content.

How do you blend the art of storytelling with the often technical practice of targeting keywords, optimizing pages for search engines, and so on?

We've found that it helps to work in two phases. Get the story on paper first and hone the message of what we're trying to say. Then work on the aspects of search engine optimization and such. This way by the time we get to the technical phase, we have already worked out the creative process.

Does the B Impact Assessment play into your content marketing efforts at all? If so, how?

We recently launched a campaign called "Measure What Matters" which lifts the B Impact Assessment into it's own campaign and brings on a series of workshops in different cities for people to get acquainted with the Assessment. We will be launching a separate website for Measure What Matters this fall. We have made adjustments in our social media strategy to account for these additions and to promote them accordingly.

What's your favorite technique for translating the somewhat complicated story of B Corps to the "500 words or less" format of the web?

We've conducted several years of consumer research to see which taglines and verbiage resonate most with the public. Asking for user feedback has been key on condensing and streamlining the complexity of our story.

How do you promote your content? How do you measure the success of each promotion?

For digital community-wide initiatives, we utilize the collective reach of all 800+ B Corporations. Together, all B Corps reach more than 20 Million followers on social media. We plan and executive collaborated postings, interactions, and launches for new campaigns.

B Lab has done a great job at building community in the business world. How do you extend that idea to your virtual properties, like your blog, website, and social networks?

One very effective tool we have built is a private social group to bring together the Digital Directors/Social Media Managers of all B Corps to talk to each other, collaborate, bounce ideas, and support each other. Virtual camaraderie is just as important as in-person camaraderie, and we have found that the two help to fuel each other. We have also recently launched a private social group to bring together the Employees of all B Corps to share best practices and share their stories with each other of working for different B Corps.

How do you measure success in your content marketing efforts? How do you improve upon that success?

We have honed and greatly improved our usage of Universal Analytics to measure visitor traffic, demographics, amounts of time that users spend on specific web pages and pieces of content, as well as effectiveness of content, bounce rates, and percentage exits. We also collect analytics from all of our social media channels to measure how many users interact with each piece of content. Collecting this data is vital for us to hit goals, set new goals, and compare the success rates of one piece of content over another.

Has analyzing your content or website performance resulted in any critical shifts in organizational thinking or a change in your approach to content marketing? If so, how?

Universal Analytics has been incredibly helpful for us in examining every aspect of how users interact with our websites—specifically down to things like which keywords people most commonly search for on our site—to which buttons people most commonly click. When we see pages and links that are not highly utilized by users, we can redesign that content to be more effective.

What is your loftiest content marketing goal for the next year or two?

In January 2014 we are launching a consumer campaign called B the Change. It will bring together key individuals from a group of B Corps to be the B the Change Creative Team and shepherd the next chapter of our evolution, as we grow from a community of companies to a movement of people.

Are there any lessons you have learned that you would like to share about B Lab's content marketing efforts?

Since the digital space is constantly evolving, with new social networks and new tools launching around the clock, we have found that flexibility is vital. We are constantly adapting to new platforms, and this has been key to staying fresh in such a fast paced industry of social and technological innovation.

Notes

1. Giselle Abramovich, "15 Stats Brands Should Know About Online Video," Digiday, April 3, 2013, http://digiday.com/brands/celtra-15-must-know-stats-for-online-video/.
2. Invodo, Emarketer, 2013, www.invodo.com/resources/statistics.
3. WVMP, "The Power of Online Video—The Stats 2013," August 19, 2013, http://webvideomarket ingportugal.com/the-power-of-online-video-the-stats-2013/.

CHAPTER EIGHT

Content and Social Networks

People use social media to keep tabs on their friends, talk about their interests, learn new things, find cool events, music, ideas, products, and so on. Companies use social media to promote their services and products. Sadly, many companies think far more about the latter and less about the former, leading to a widening gap between the interests of these two groups. Plus, with networks like Facebook offering higher news feed priority to promoted posts (i.e., ads), the challenge of reaching a target audience with custom content and creating meaningful online relationships organically has become more difficult.

In this chapter we'll push beyond hustling for Likes and Retweets and think more about how you can use social tools to collaborate, engage, and build community. We will share examples of killer social media content campaigns in two categories: engagement and promotion. Then, we close with a few pointers about ways to maximize your organization's use of several popular social networks.

Engaging Community

As with content on our blog and website, we generally try to follow the 80/20 rule on social networks too (80% value-driven content vs. 20% promotion). It doesn't always boil down to firm percentages and nicely portioned pie charts, however, because there is a fair bit of overlap between content for promotion and engagement. The entire point of successful content strategy is to create content that meets both organizational goals and those of your audience.

On social networks, you also have more interpersonal interaction on shared content through comments, wall posts, shares, retweets, and so on, meaning it is not just about what you create that adds value but also about how you interact in useful and meaningful ways. Thus, identifying unique ideas, facts, and other things you can contribute to the conversation will go a long way in helping you build and maintain a thriving community. It is much more useful to have a legion of super fans in a community-based ecosystem that takes care of its own than simply a list of customers, even if they are repeat customers.

Because your organization's unique value proposition is different from all the others (that's the point, right?), there is no way to write up a set of foolproof step-by-step instructions for creating engaging content that will work for everyone who reads this book. That's where concrete examples can help. Here are some common types of successful content campaigns illustrated with examples of organizations doing it right.

Pique Interest: The Field Museum of Chicago

The easiest way to engage people is to pique their interest with an interesting story or picture. The Field Museum capitalizes on their unique asset: the vaults. Every week their social media team pulls something fascinating from their vaults, snaps its picture, and tells its story.

Figure 8.1

Inspire: UNICEF

Inspirational messages have been the currency of the internet since the days of email forwarding. UNICEF shares topical and beautiful photos that both inspire their readers and underscore the importance of the UNICEF mission.

Figure 8.2

Peer Gratitude: Donor's Choose

Giving shout outs to peers in the field takes 60 seconds and fills them with a warm, happy glow.

Figure 8.3

Customer/Donor/Member Gratitude: Diabetes U.K.

Diabetes U.K. uses 7-second Vine videos to thank individual donors. These mini-videos are incredibly lo-fi—they probably took less than 5 minutes to create from start to finish—but they show their donors that every contribution matters.

Figure 8.4

Compliment Customers/ Members: Toms Shoes

Toms Shoes further endears themselves to a dedicated fan base by sharing photos of customers looking stylin' in their shoes.

Figure 8.5

Crowdsource: EarthShare Member's Project Board

The EarthShare Members' Projects board on Pinterest showcases the projects of member charities. This strategy of empowering members to contribute to a group board could be employed by any member-based organization, such as a chamber of commerce, community foundations with numerous grantees, a state tourism office that promotes many cities and regions, consortia of museums or a group of zoos and aquariums who want to informally work together to promote ocean conservancy.

Figure 8.6

Comment on Current Events: Oreo

Oreo frequently pairs a gorgeous photo and a social message to comment on an event, a tactic that has won them over 26 million fans on Facebook. This Pride cookie remains one of their most shared, liked, and commented on images.

Figure 8.7

Entertain: PETA2

PETA2 provokes laughter and action by pairing surprising images with emotional appeals. This is a great example of taking advantage of the psychological reasons people share content, in this case because they are laughing at funny cat pictures.

Figure 8.8

Give Aways: Nature Conservancy

The Nature Conservancy doesn't stop at just creating gorgeous photos—they give them away as wallpaper.

Figure 8.9

Donor Circles: Heart-Shaped World

Pinterest group boards can be used to facilitate donors circles, encouraging like-minded donors to share causes they are supporting with each other.

Figure 8.10

Figure 8.11

Content Curation: Stanford's Center for Social Innovation

The Center for Social Innovation at the Stanford Graduate School of Business scans the internet and academia to find the most interesting, well-researched and provocative new ideas on social innovation and publishes them on its Twitter feed, @SocInnovators, which has nearly 44,000 followers.

Eye Candy: Rails-to-Trails Conservancy

The Rails-to-Trails mission is to transform abandoned rail lines into hiking and biking trails. RTC publishes a daily photo of a gorgeous rail-trail somewhere in the United States.

Figure 8.12

Continue the Conversation: Rio+20 Earth Summit

The Future We Want[1] board was created to enable participants in the Project Based Rio+20 Earth Summit to continue the conversation after the conclusion of the summit, and to expand the conversation to organizations that weren't able to attend in person. This board has over 100 global collaborators, including the United Nations and UNICEF, the Rainforest Alliance, and regional offices of Greenpeace and the World Wildlife Fund.

Figure 8.13

Engage Donors Around Campaigns: Oxfam

Oxfam created a Pinterest board around the theme of their GROW campaign, supporting the growth of sustainable agriculture, by inviting their followers to contribute summer recipes featuring produce grown using GROW methods.

Figure 8.14

Promoting Your Content

Engaging your audience through interesting content and freebies is a great use of social media, but you can also directly promote your business. In this section, we look at using social media that supports direct calls to action.

A good rule of thumb for content creation is to spend about half your time creating killer content and the other half figuring out how to cleverly promote it across all your channels. This approach will help ensure that the time and effort spent on audience research and content creation doesn't get wasted because no one actually found the gorgeous stuff you created.

Again, your organization's optimal promotion strategy depends on your offer and your audience, so we've created a list of promotional content types paired with examples to kick off your brainstorming.

Match People to Offers: ASPCA, Animal Planet, and the Humane Society

On this board, the ASPCA, the Humane Society of the United States and Animal Planet worked together to promote animals that need to be rescued.

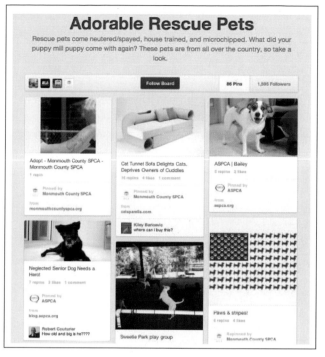

Figure 8.15

Organize: GLAAD

GLAAD keeps track of gay and lesbian issues and organizes social actions, like petitions and write-in campaigns. They then create gorgeous images their supporters can share with their own networks, like the one below. Posts with photos or graphics and shared links generally tend to perform better than those with just links.

Figure 8.16

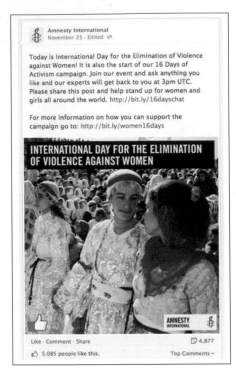

Figure 8.17.1

Educate: Amnesty International

Amnesty International organizes Facebook chats to answer questions and raise awareness about issues. In the examples here, they promote the session over time with a range of images.

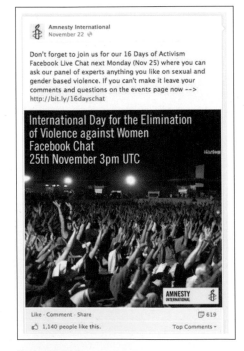

Figure 8.17.2

Figure 8.17.3

Deals: LocalvoreVT

Localvore Vermont curates deals on local, sustainable products.

Figure 8.18

Buy/Donate: Ahambhumika

Ahambhumika added emotional weight to their clear call to action with a photo showing a family who benefited from their campaign last year.

Figure 8.19

Share Expertise: Hubspot

Hubspot is an inbound marketing software platform. They add value to their customers and tempt potential new customers by sharing their expertise in the form of tips and resources to help organizations improve their digital marketing.

Figure 8.20

Report: Charity Water

Charity Water used an Instagram video to report on the impact their program had on the women of Engereda village.

Figure 8.21

Invite: 350.org

350.org not only uses channels like Facebook, Twitter and Pinterest to invite people to their events, they provide a platform for their members to organize their own.

Figure 8.22

Channel-Specific Content

In this section, we'll cover a few useful things to know about using Pinterest, Google+, Twitter and Facebook to your best advantage.

Pinterest

Pinterest makes it easy for people to share their favorite photos or "pins" with friends and is one of the most rapidly growing social media networks in the United States.[2] Pinterest offers great ways to share visual content but it can be used to collaborate as well.

Pinterest group boards curated by networks of like-minded individuals or nonprofit organizations can be used to raise awareness about a cause, cross-promote the activities of member organizations in a consortium, facilitate donors circles, or to promote many businesses or organizations in a geographic area.

Why Use Pinterest to Collaborate?

There are numerous benefits for non-profits to collaborate on a Pinterest board created around a specific topic, cause, or giving campaign:

- It doesn't require a lot of time to maintain. Pinning a photo or article takes about a minute once you've installed a Pin It button in your browser.
- Collaborating with other organizations reduces the burden on any one organization to publish a lot of content.
- Pinterest can aggregate many types of content about a single topic in a single board including: blog posts, news articles, photos, videos (YouTube and Vimeo videos can be viewed without leaving Pinterest), quotations and infographics.
- Repinning another organization's content, posting it to Facebook or to Twitter is a snap with handy *Like*, *Tweet* and *Embed on my Blog* buttons that appear alongside every pin. Hashtags work on Pinterest as well.

Google+

Having a Facebook brand page should not be the end of your social strategy. Ensuring that you have a Google+ presence and that your fans can easily share content so that that social capital can be translated into increased brand awareness is essential. Love it or hate it, there are two key reasons why Google+ should figure prominently in your content promotion efforts

1. Search Results

Google's social network crystallizes the need for a comprehensive social strategy to complement search optimization efforts. Logged in users will have the option to see personalized results, and results that are specific to one's Google+ connections. Also, finding people and profiles will be easier with Google+ pages appearing in both results and in autocomplete. As Google notes on their blog, "because behind most every query is a community." Be sure to claim your brand page(s) on Google+, as claimed brand pages now show up prominently in search results.

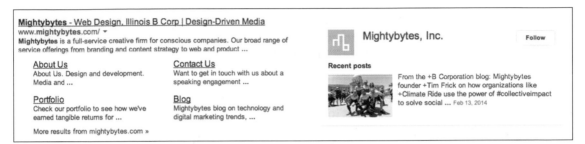

Figure 8.23 Here's our Mightybytes Google+ brand page, complete with photo of Tim on Climate Ride.

2. Google Authorship

We talked about claiming brand pages above, but what about claiming personal pages? Google Authorship is a great way to increase your authority as a content creator in search results. Research has shown that results with photos tend to get higher click-through rates than those without. Connecting your Google+ page will allow your profile picture to show up on posts you've written. This is done simply by adding a link to your Google+ page to posts created on various sites or blogs. Here's an example from Tim's account:

<a title = "Author: Tim Frick on Google+" rel = "author" href = "https://plus. google.com/u/0/+TimFrick/" target = "_blank">Google+</a>

I put this in every guest post I can, and in search results it shows up like this:

Figure 8.24

Twitter

Here are our top five tips for maximizing content effectiveness on the world's largest microblogging platform.

1. Don't Max Out Your Character Limit

The little blue birdie gives you a mere 140 characters in which to tweet, so keeping entries at 125 characters or less will allow others to easily re-tweet (RT) your

Photos consistently perform better on Facebook than plain-text comments or links, but with important updates, it's a good idea to scatter some advertising into the mix to "boost" your content so it reaches the max number of followers.

Conclusion

As of this writing, Pinterest, Google+, Twitter, and Facebook are in the top tier of social media platforms, but that doesn't mean they are the only four worth integrating into your social media strategy. For example, web development companies can connect with developers on Github.com and recruiters can connect with potential candidates on LinkedIn. The user research techniques we covered in earlier strategy chapters can help you uncover the optimal social media platforms for your organization.

What we covered:

- Examples of social content that has improved target audience engagement.
- Examples of successful content promotion efforts on social networks.
- Channel-specific guidelines for social media content.

Profile

Figure 8.27 Mana Ionescu is the President of Lightspan Digital

Mana Ionescu
President, Lightspan Digital
Mana Ionescu, President of Lightspan Digital, shares her thoughts about the role that metrics plays in social media strategy, about how to maximize your social efforts and about the importance of empathy.

Lightspan Digital (http://lightspandigital.com/) tells brands' stories, helps connect target audiences with their clients' services and products through social media, content marketing and more. In addition to running the company, Mana is also a speaker, and passionate SCUBA Diver on track to become an instructor. Mana wants to teach about the ocean experience, and how we can give life back to the ocean instead of taking it away.

What's the one critical skill an online marketer needs in today's ever-evolving world of content, search and social?

Critical thinking—today's marketers need to be able to collect varied and seemingly disparate data points and information and discern what works, what doesn't, and how to build better marketing scenarios based on this knowledge. Another skill is empathy. Particularly social media marketing, it is about people. It's much closer to sales and customers service than creative marketing. It requires empathy.

How does Lightspan Digital measure success with clients?

We look at more data than we have use for. Everything from clicks per follower on Facebook, to average sales ticket from Pinterest vs. Facebook. We even look at percentage conversion from each blog post. We tailor the measurements to the objectives. But ultimately the most universal and revealing data is traffic to the point of conversion and conversion rates where possible.

For one of our ecommerce clients, we know that Facebook pushes the most traffic to the website, but the average ticket is lower than Twitter and Pinterest conversions. So while we get less traffic from Twitter and Pinterest, those who visit have a higher intention to buy and spend more. This tells us that if we can increase the volume of traffic from Twitter and Pinterest, all else staying the same, with that alone we should be able to increase revenue.

We also look at increase in database contacts. Particularly with B2B companies, we look to fill the top of the funnel with targeted contacts. Some call those leads, I prefer to call them contacts because typically they require additional qualification. So the measurements here would be—increase in traffic to the website and increase in contacts collection.

How do you determine which metrics matter and which don't?

This takes a whole lot of testing and learning. We now have almost four years of data across hundreds of campaigns, so we are able to see what's a consistent pattern and what's a spike or dip to be concerned with. We're not too concerned with slow-downs in Facebook follower growth, for example, but if traffic coming to the website from Facebook slows down, we then look to see what needs to be adjusted.

A lot of the data repeats itself and is irrelevant. Twitter reach for example, is irrelevant—it's an estimate of how many people could have seen your message if they were all on Twitter at the same time, and all paying attention just to you. So a reach estimate of 10,000 could have actually been 1 or 9,999. The margin of error is so large the data is not to be trusted.

Most businesses can track everything they need in Universal Analytics by making sure they source code all URLs used on social networks (using the google url builder tool). Same as PPC campaign.

Also B2B companies need to start tracking the sources of their referrals. I am blown away by how many still don't have a proper sales process. You will always run your marketing blindly if you don't know exactly how many referrals you get from your website a year, vs. your strategic partners, vs. your speaking engagements etc. Before pointing the finger at social media, B2B companies should put in place a solid sales tracking process. Adding social media a referral source will then be easy as pie.

Any Universal Analytics tips?

We keep Universal Analytics annotations for all marketing events, which helps us track back any spikes to the work done. When analytics is done rigorously, mysteries are rare.

How do you develop promotional strategies for sharing content to maximize impact?

We call our method "leaving footprints everywhere and making sure they all clearly lead back to us." We were working on promoting a documentary about a famous New York artist. We found a Flickr album from one of her exhibits at MoMA. Although a couple of years old, the album was still getting comments daily. This fan base was still active so it seemed like the perfect place to announce the release of the documentary. We left a comment with a link to the website. We left comments like that all over the web. And articles and Facebook and Twitter posts. The Flickr comment drove the most clicks to the website. Within a day we had 700 visitors just from that one comment. Overall the traffic to the documentary page was off the charts. All those footprints added up to quite a successful influx of visitors.

When we work with YouTube videos we embed links in the videos themselves to lead to a point of conversion. Infographics have captions with links to "learn more." Every piece of content is designed to lead back to the homebase and the homebase is designed to convince and convert.

How do keywords factor into a successful effort to share content?

We always look to rank high in search results, regardless of type of content. We've worked with film promos on YouTube, and the smarter we were about the keywords the more views we got. So we tackle every campaign the same way—the content needs to be not only developed but also promoted. So whether it's text or images or video, we look to execute the content development and the content promotion perfectly.

What are your general recommendations for keyword research and usage on a piece of web content?

Start with keywords and trends research. You can use Ubersuggest or other tools such as SEO Moz to determine ideal keywords. Then check their competitiveness. Then write, let creativity flow.

What about hashtags?

Hashtags are a science on their own. We say that for every hour of content production, spend another hour editing and then a day promoting it. That's where the hashtags come in. It's good to use a mix of descriptive and trending hashtags. Use no more than two per post and keep using them to highlight the topic of your post as well as to show associations with other topics.

Ultimately, you can't have hashtags without content and you can't have social media promotion without hashtags. So you'll need to work on both.

How do you get your clients to move beyond the blog post to incorporate other forms of content such as graphics, video and audio?

We tell our clients—show don't tell. From the beginning of times until the end of times, humans will be "painting" pictures. Whether through words, infographics, music videos, or a combination of these, you have to tell your story. Not what you sell. But who you are. That part of you that makes you extraordinary, that part of you that makes you loveable and memorable. You want to make people say, "I love that guy or I love that gal." Then and only then will they buy from you over and over again.

Do you have any specific thoughts on content creation vs. content curation?

I think they both have their place. I just recommend curation with a commentary. It becomes more of a dialogue if you can comment on a piece of content you find valuable. Dialogue leads to relationships. Relationships lead to sales. Curation without commentary is copycat. There's no value in that.

In your opinion, what are the shared disciplines between the fields of UX, marketing, or content strategy?

They all start with the same fundamental question of, "what does my customer need to feel like their time spent with me/my brand was worthwhile?"

Where are they distinctly different?

They differ in which problems we are capable of solving. As a digital marketer, I don't have the skills or experience to design a user experience flow. In fact, designing is the last thing you'd want me to do. But I can get people to visit that page and go through that experience. And content marketing will tell the compelling story that will turn a visitor from curious bystander to interested buyer.

Notes

1. Pinterest, "The Future We Want," www.pinterest.com/worldresources/future-we-want-post-2015-rio%2B20-earth-summit-riopl/.
2. Alison Griswald, "Pinterest Is Now the Fastest Growing Content-Sharing Platform," November 5, 2013, www.businessinsider.com/pinterest-is-fastest-growing-content-sharing-platform-2013-11.
3. Cooper Smith, "The Planet's 24 Largest Social Media Sites, And Where Their Next Wave Of Growth Will Come From," Business Insider, November 29, 2013, www.businessinsider.com/a-global-social-media-census-2013-10.
4. Josh Constine, "Facebook Reveals 78% Of US Users Are Mobile As It Starts Sharing User Counts By Country," Techcrunch, August 13, 2013, http://techcrunch.com/2013/08/13/facebook-mobile-user-count/.

CHAPTER NINE

Creating Usable Designs

Good design is one of the most important ways to instill confidence in online visitors. Your site, your blog, mobile apps, and customization of social media profiles should all adhere to professional design standards that communicate credibility, reliability, expertise and consistency across media types and platforms. You have a split second to make a good first impression and few things will drive a potential new customer away from your site faster than bad design.

"A successful ambassador or salesperson will arrive with excellent references and present a sparkling, well-dressed appearance," Loveday and Niehaus note in their book *Web Design for ROI.* "A landing page can do the same through design, function, and visible references."

In this chapter we cover tools and processes for designing digital interfaces that integrate content, usability and visual design.

Andrew B. King, author of the very informative *Website Optimization* from O'Reilly, cites credibility-based, professional design as the number one factor in maximizing site conversion rates. He defines the core criteria of credibility-based design as:

1. **Speed.** If your site doesn't load and react quickly you will lose customers.
2. **Reliability.** If it spits back errors in spelling, facts, code, style, or grammar you will lose customers.
3. **Attractiveness.** If the visual design detracts from, rather than supports, the information presented you will—you guessed it—lose customers.

We add a fourth:

4. **Ease-of-use.** If a site isn't easy to use and the content or products on it easy to find, you will also lose customers. Thus, *site usability and navigation* are equally important to customer site (and subsequently brand) loyalty.

Creating Wireframes and Prototypes

So much information about goals, technology, and content must be integrated into digital design that cross-team wireframe and prototype workshops are the best way to keep everyone on the same page.

Wireframes

Website wireframes are blueprints that show how navigation and interface elements are displayed on site pages. Their purpose is to establish user interface functionality before visual design and development begins. There are two basic types of wireframes:

- **Low-fidelity wireframes** define navigation and basic site structure. These are reviewed first and don't typically define interactions or the weight of elements on a page.
- **High-fidelity wireframes** define a page's visual hierarchy and typically include labels, form elements, instructional text, and so on. They attempt to define all interactions and product details with the goal of providing enough information that visual designers and engineers can begin their work.

Though wireframes are typically created by user experience designers, team input is critical for overall project success:

- Marketing and analytics experts can ensure that layouts align with the site's business goals and ability to benchmark success.
- Content strategists can ensure that interface elements support site messaging and overall content integrity.
- Visual designers can have input on migrating wireframes to visual design.
- Front-end developers can identify any elements that may be difficult to code and recommend alternatives.
- Back-end developers can identify any elements that require changes to the databases and third-party plug-ins the site runs on.

Creating Wireframes

The most efficient way to develop wireframes is to start with low-fidelity sketches and end with a detailed blueprint. A sketching session using pen and paper or a whiteboard offers a quick and simple way to brainstorm ideas and get stakeholders in agreement on the layout of key screens for a project interface. From hand-drawn sketches, wireframes evolve to high-fidelity layouts that nail down interface specifics for all content types, including logos, search fields, navigation, imagery, calls-to-action, text boxes and so on. By the time high-fidelity wireframes have been approved by all

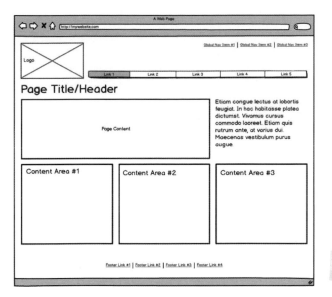

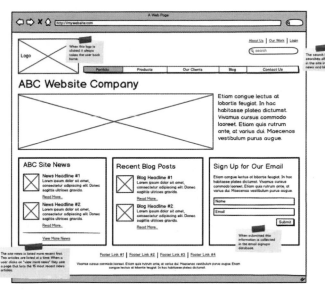

Figure 9.1 and 9.2 Low-fidelity wireframes are used to define the structure of a site, while high-fidelity wireframes are blueprints that visual designers and developers use to build the site.

Pattern Libraries

Design patterns are solutions for common website design requirements like menus, search boxes, blogs, galleries, headers and footers. They enable designers to build on best practices in site design rather than starting from scratch for every single element. Design patterns range from simple screen shots to templates that include front-end code.

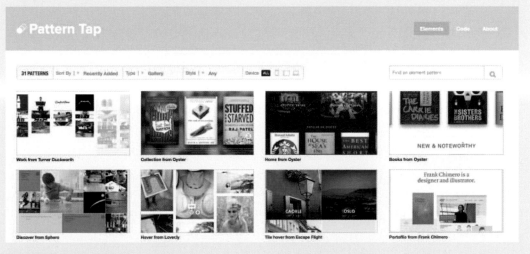

Figure 9.3 Pattern libraries curate design solutions for common web design elements.

Our favorite pattern libraries include:

- Welie.com
- Patterny.com
- Patterntap.com
- Uipatterns.com
- Pttrns.com

key stakeholders, a visual designer should have no problem translating them to completed design comps for implementation by developers.

Sketching Low-Fi Wireframes

Try these basic steps to kick-off a collaborative design brainstorm session in which low-fi wireframe sketches are the outcome:

1. **Context:** Kick off the session with a 2-minute "elevator pitch" that describes the goal of the site, the audiences you anticipate serving, and the navigation chart. Identify the pages you plan to build wireframes for during this session.
2. **Sketch:** Each person at the table should sketch out at least two sets of wireframes for the pages. Sketching two ensures that everyone keeps an open mind about the end goal rather than getting too invested in their own idea.
3. **Vote:** Each person at the table should review the sketches and vote up elements that they like on the sketches.
4. **Discuss:** Starting with the elements people voted on, discuss the pros and cons of various approaches. Each person should primarily share insights from their own expertise: meeting business goals, keeping the site on budget, etc.
5. **Frankenstein:** Create a sketch that contains the best elements. Call an end to the meeting.
6. **Decide:** Work up a high fidelity wireframe (see below) based on your Frankenstein, vote to move forward or change it.

If stakeholders cannot agree on low-fi wireframes, it can sometimes be helpful to create a paper prototype to identify potential strengths and weaknesses in planned task flows. See the sidebar on Paper Prototypes vs. Digital for more information.

High-Fidelity Wireframes

Unlike low-fidelity wireframes, which are typically just rough sketches, high-fidelity wireframes offer a complete blueprint of primary screens with all key interface components in place. User experience designers typically create these deliverables using software-based tools (see sidebar on Wireframing Tools). By the time high-fidelity wireframes are approved, all stakeholders should be in agreement on *placement* of all key interface elements, leaving little room for "creative interpretation" on the part of

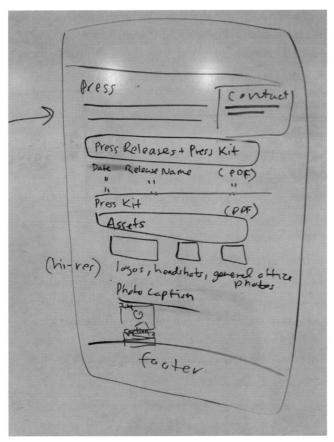

Figure 9.4 The result of the Mightybytes.com Press page sketch session.

Figure 9.5 The Press page visual comp our designers created based on the team wireframe collaboration session.

Why Prototype?

Here are a few benefits of creating and testing prototypes before advancing to the build stage:

1. **Prototypes help you identify user issues before the site—or even the site structure—is complete**. It's cheap and easy to revise task flows and site navigation when the process is a matter of rearranging sheets of paper or changing the links on a clickable prototype; it's much more difficult to swap out functions or steps in a task flow when the site is nearly complete.

2. **Prototypes surface practical challenges**. By making site concepts concrete, prototypes surface practical questions that can easily be overlooked in the "big picture" design process. For example, if users get lost on their way to a piece of content, can they find their way back?

3. **Prototypes test visual layout**. Tree tests are a terrific tool for ensuring that your navigation is intuitive, but prototypes test both navigation and wireframe design. Most site visitors rely on a combination of visual elements and text to find their way around a site, so testing them together can make a big difference.

Prototypes do require extra time and resources, so teams should plan accordingly during strategy sessions and budgeting. They are most valuable for the sections of apps and websites that require users to go through a complicated set of steps. For example, for a library website you might create a prototype to show the workflow for a person searching the catalogue and putting a book on hold, but not a person reading the blog.

Paper Prototypes vs. Digital

Paper prototypes are quick, easy, and cost-effective. All you have to do is create paper wireframes outlining a website or task flow process and ask prospective users to point (literally, with their finger) to a button, then asking them where said button might take them. They're a down-n-dirty, quick way to get multiple stakeholders on the same page about common website functions.

However, as they aren't truly interactive, paper prototypes can lead to many misunderstandings of functionality and requirements, especially if the project requires a complicated set of tasks from users. Sometimes a digital prototype is more effective. There are plenty of software and cloud-based tools that can help you generate clickable prototypes:

- Balsamiq.com
- Creately.com
- Pidoco.com
- Lumzy.com
- gliffy.com
- HotGloo: www.hotgloo.com/
- ProtoShare: www.protoshare.com/
- Axure: www.axure.com/

Budget and timeline will likely drive which of the above options is right for your project. The goal for each approach is the same: simplify common user processes and drive a common understanding of navigation and functionality for site stakeholders.

Sketching for Interactive Design

Once functionality is established through wireframing and, if applicable prototyping, plan out the interactive design of your website or application. Depending on the site or product being created, you may need to wireframe or prototype multiple screens or task flows to get the buy-in of all stakeholders.

Sketching Adaptive or Responsive Design

As you no doubt recall from Chapter 4, a responsive website design will fluidly adapt to any screen size, while an adaptive website design is a set of fixed designs for pre-defined screen sizes. In both cases, designers are creating interfaces for a range of screen sizes. For sketching purposes, however, responsive and adaptive designs are approached the same way: designers create visual comps only for the primary screen sizes. Creating a full set of visual comps for all the screen sizes a responsive site could adapt to would be prohibitively time consuming!

The purpose of these visual comps is two-fold:

1. Define the logic of how the CSS will change the look of the page across devices.
2. Ensure that the ideas are workable across your team:
   - Copywriters do a "writer's rough" to ensure copy fits.
   - Interactive or user experience designers check for good user flow.
   - Front end developers ensure the design can be coded in time, on budget and for a top quality user experience.
   - Back end developers identify all necessary 3rd party integrations, databases, and content fields necessary to support the visual design.
   - Visual designers get direction on the design logic and parameters.

When Mightybytes implemented a responsive website redesign, we created just two sets of visual comps: mobile phone and desktop. We chose these two because they represented the biggest difference in screen size, which enabled us to identify new content needs as well as any places where the visual design would need to change to improve page speed or legibility.

Sketching Touch Interfaces for Mobile and Tablet

Touch interface design is primarily based on understanding where people's fingers tend to naturally come to rest on mobile devices. Then there are additional design principles for mobile and tablet design that take slower internet speeds, portability, smaller screens and touch interface functionality into account.

Ultimately, interface design for mobile phones and tablets begins with the same principles as desktop design: know your user, understand their goals, and make it as easy as possible for them to take the action they are at the site to take.

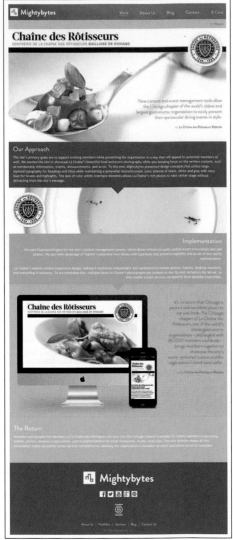

Figure 9.8 and 9.9 These two visual comps defined exactly how the Mightybytes Portfolio page would look on both desktop and mobile devices.

Mobile Touch Interface Guidelines

Figure 9.10 People tend to navigate their mobile phones using one of these three positions, a tendency that should inform your interface design.

1. Put navigation controls at the bottom of the device.

As you can see in the sketch above, people tend to use their phones one handed; they hold their phones in their palm and use their thumb to navigate their mobile devices. This habit, known as "bottom screen bias," results in design phone interfaces with the most important navigation options at the bottom of the screen. This "bottom-screen bias" is much more important than any left/right hand differences because most people can easily switch hands as necessary. The screens in Figure 9.11 are good examples of "bottom-screen bias."

2. Separate touchscreen and phone controls

Where possible, put your touchscreen navigation controls on the opposite side of the phone's controls. This is easy to do when you're building an app specifically for an iPhone or an Android but harder to plan for on a web page's mobile display, since you have no way of knowing what device your readers are using to access your page. Pattern libraries can help you find the right solution for your web page.

3. Make buttons as big as you can

Keep in mind that buttons are tapped by people with a variety of physical characteristics. User finger size, vision impairments, physical disabilities, and a host of other traits should be taken into consideration when designing interface elements. The bare minimum button size for mobile phones is 44 × 44 pixels, but they should be as big as you can make them without compromising integrity of the design.

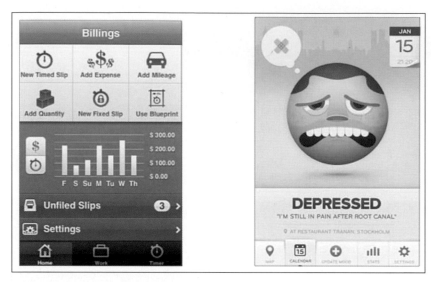

Figure 9.11 These two mobile interfaces were designed to make it easy for people to action with their thumbs.

Figure 9.12 This shows how one site designed its app interface for Android and iPhone. Notice that the app navigation bar is at the top of the interface for the Android phone and at the bottom for the iPhone.

Figure 9.13 From left to right: Apple phone dial screen, Chase bank, and Instagram. All three mobile phone interfaces were designed to be easy to use for people with fat fingers and poor eyesight!

Here are three designs for a mobile phone interface that show how all three principles fit together.

Tablets Touch Interface Guidelines

People tend to hold bigger tablets by the top third of the device with their fingers supporting the back, which means that their thumbs can most easily reach navigation controls in the corners.

1. Put navigation controls in the corner

As you can see in Figure 9.14 people tend to hold their tablets in such a way that makes it easiest to take action by tapping on the corners of the devices. As a result, designers typically put navigation controls either in the top corners or in menus that appear in the margins towards the top of the screen. See Figure 9.15 for an example.

2. Put browsing controls beneath the content display window

Whenever controls display or affect content, they should be placed to the side or below that content so the user's hand doesn't block their view. See Figure 9.16 for an example.

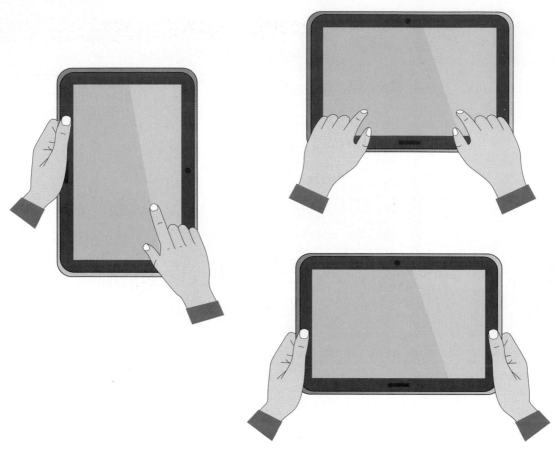

Figure 9.14 People tend to navigate their tablets using one of these three positions, a fact that should influence your tablet interface design.

3. Choose a primary tablet orientation

All tablet devices can be used in both landscape and portrait mode, which adds another layer of decision making to the interface design. As ever, the content of your site should dictate your choice of primary orientation. News sites, for example, tend to be used primarily in portrait orientation and sites with prominent video players tend to be used primarily in landscape orientation.

Designing for Page Speed

Speed is one of the defining criteria in a credible website. In a 2009 study[1] done by Forrester Research and Akamai, it was revealed that 47% of customers expect a website to load in 2 seconds or less and 40% of shoppers will wait no more than

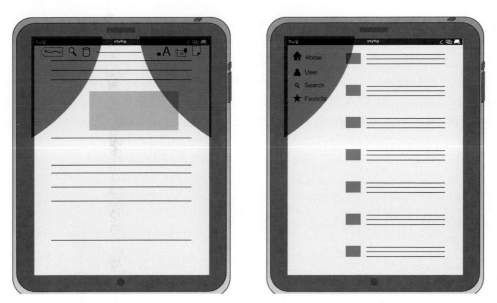

Figure 9.15 Putting the navigation controls in the corner of tablet interfaces makes it easy for users to take action.

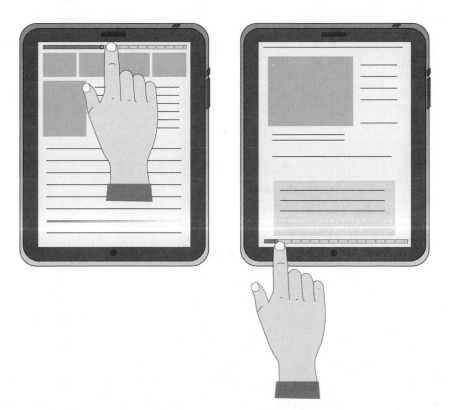

Figure 9.16 Put browsing controls below content so that people can browse without blocking their view.

508-Compliance

Section 508 was a 1986 amendment to the Rehabilitation Act of 1973, created to eliminate barriers to electronic and information technology for people with disabilities. It was completely revised in 1998 to accommodate growth in the industry and recognize significant technology shifts. The law applies to all federal agencies that develop and maintain websites or online content of any kind.

Even though your organization may not be a federal agency, addressing Section 508 disability guidelines should be considered a minimal approach to creating a great site experience for users with disabilities. The compliance guidelines provide a lowest common denominator guideline, but don't set the bar very high. Shoot for exceeding user expectations, not falling short of them.

For full details on Section 508 site compliance for users with disabilities, check out the website at: www.section509.gov/

3 seconds before abandoning a retail or travel site. The study also found that after a poor site experience:

- 79% of dissatisfied shoppers are less likely to buy from an online site again
- 27% are less likely to buy from that retailer *off-line.*
- Customer loyalty is tied closely to how quickly a website loads (especially true for high-spending shoppers).
- 44% would actively tell their friends and family about the bad experience.

While the study was based on commerce-driven websites, these concepts are equally important for content-driven websites: a site that loads quickly is tantamount to maintaining customer loyalty. This is doubly important in the age of smartphones, tablets, and other internet-enabled devices.

Each page of your site should load within just a couple seconds for the majority of users and be instantly responsive once loaded. This includes text, images, code, and any interactive elements. Everyone wants a fast and rewarding internet experience, so make certain you give them one. Analyze every portion of every page on your site to be sure they adhere to user standards for speed across devices, browsers and platforms. This is important not only for users but for energy use as well. The faster files download from your website the less energy they use, which is a more sustainable long-term strategy.

Media Optimization

Website media elements—animation, video, games, and so on—will take up the lion's share of a user's bandwidth, so make their experience worthwhile. Rich media has the potential to engage users like few other things on your site. It also has the potential to annoy them with long download times and unsupported file formats, not to mention using unnecessary energy for things they don't ultimately want. Make sure all copy associated with these content types is clear and appropriately labeled so users have a clear understanding of what they download.

Optimize all media files for speedy download using standard compression tools. Consider that Flash files—long the gold standard of rich media—are no longer supported by many mobile devices.

Optimize each element following the same quality-performance standards you set for site graphics—balancing quality with speed and performance. Audio, Flash, and video files should load as quickly as possible and look great.

- Use a format that's widely adopted by site visitors and supported on mobile devices.
- No autostart for video and audio files! Use a clickable thumbnail instead.
- If possible, break large files into small manageable chunks to decrease load time.
- Run tests to ensure files play quickly upon loading.

If there's no getting around long download times, clarify expectations in as succinct a manner as possible. Users may consider waiting for a large white paper or tutorial video if expectations are managed properly. Just remember to measure performance for this large document and dump it if performance doesn't meet expectations.

Design Asset Optimization

Performance optimization is primarily in the realm of developers, but designers and content strategists can get in on the act too by optimizing content and design assets for mobile devices first.

Here are some techniques for optimizing design assets:

1. Use CSS Sprites

CSS sprites combine multiple images or graphics into a single image to maximize page speed and minimize HTTP requests. This is especially useful when applied to navigation items or other elements that are repeated in multiple places across a site. All navigation items are combined into a single image, which is optimized for speedy web delivery and downloaded by a browser only once. CSS is then used to display only the portion of an image necessary to serve a particular navigational purpose.

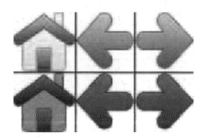

Figure 9.17 This is a CSS sprite for a simple navigation with just three options: home, left and right. The sprite contains 6 total images: a standard navigation image for home, left and right and a "rollover state," which shows what the navigation button looks like when the mouse is hovering over it. Combining all 6 possible options in one image maximizes page speed because the sprite has to be downloaded only once for each of the 6 options to show, rather than download requiring a separate download for each option.

2. Optimize Image File Types

When you create an image and then save it for the web, compression occurs and your file gets smaller. Different file types take different approaches to reducing file size. Selecting the correct type of file for a particular image will often result in a smaller file size.

- Use JPEGs for photographs and illustrations with extensive gradients or shading.

- Use GIF or SVG for vector images or line art to maintain image clarity along with small file size.
- For images that need to stay crisp while supporting partial transparency, use the PNG file format.

If you use Adobe products such as Photoshop, you can use the "Save for the Web" interface to preview your image saved as different file types. Figure 9.18 was created by selecting the "4 up" tab in the Save for the Web dialogue box, which allows us to look at four versions of the image at once.

In Figure 9.19, we have selected a JPEG file type for a photograph of cyclists on Climate Ride (see the final chapter for more info on Climate Ride). After you select a file type for an image,

Figure 9.18 This is one picture saved as four different file types with hugely different weights. By selecting the JPEG file type, you can often make the file sizes of your images smaller. In this example, you can see that by selecting the JPEG file type we were able to save 399.57 kb in comparison to the original file.

Figure 9.19 The goal of Image Optimization is to reduce your file size without reducing the quality of the image. This example from Photoshop shows the differences between the original image (top left) and the image saved at three quality levels: low, medium, and high.

you can adjust the quality of the JPEG. You're looking for the smallest file size that is visually acceptable in the proper file format.

In Figure 9.19, you can see that the low quality version of the JPEG (top right) contains digital artifacts on the yellow sign that compromise the quality of the image. The artifacts in the medium quality image (bottom left) are less noticeable, but still present. The maximum quality image has no artifacts, but is half the size of the original image. A next step might be to find a happy medium between medium and high quality. Keep in mind, that if you are targeting devices with retina displays, a higher resolution photo might be desirable.

3. Font Optimization

There are two types of fonts that can be used in a web-based design:

- **System fonts:** Common fonts, like Arial and Times New Roman, that are viewable on all types of devices, whether you have a Mac or PC, are considered system fonts. This type of font is installed by default on a computer, whether or not that computer is connected to the internet.

- **Web fonts:** Web fonts are hosted online instead of on your local computer. There are hundreds of web fonts to choose from, and designers can also create custom fonts. Two popular commercial web font options are Adobe Typekit and Google Fonts.

Adobe Typekit accounts charge an annual fee for personal accounts and a monthly fee for business accounts. These fonts tend to be of higher quality and you will find some of your favorite foundries there. With a typical download size of 11kb, Typekit has less impact on page weight than Google Fonts.

Google Fonts are free and easy to implement and offer over 600 typefaces to choose from. You only need to implement a single line of code to add them to your site. The download size of Google Web fonts is around 28kb, making it the larger of the two web font options presented here.

If you have a front-end designer on your team, you can also use a DIY method: purchasing the font you want to use and then using the CSS style @font_face to implement the font across browsers. A non-optimized DIY font face has a download size of 30.5kb, making it the largest option of the three. However, a DIY web font that is optimized can result in a smaller file size, and require fewer HTTP requests, than either of the other web font options.

There are a couple of ways that a font can impact the loading speed of your website:

- **HTTP requests:** This is a term that we use to talk about the number of requests made to a server in order to load all of the elements on a page, such as fonts, photos and videos. The more HTTP requests that you make, the slower your page loads, and the more energy is required to process all of those requests.
- **Page weight:** Page weight refers to how large a page is in megabytes or gigabytes. The smaller the page, the faster it loads, and the less energy is needed to load the page.

System fonts require the least amount of energy to load, because they are installed on local computers. However, they limit a designer's options in creating a design that is attractive and distinct.

Web fonts of all types greatly expand a designer's palette, but can increase the HTTP requests to your page and add page weight and thus affect page load time. Some sets of web fonts have a bigger impact than others.

Most web pages use a combination of both system and web fonts. For example, a web font may look great as a header, but it's probably not necessary for all the body copy, which could be rendered with a system font. By taking preventative measures while planning your site, you can save on overall page size and server load when your website launches.

4. Font Glyphs

One great way to maintain design integrity while also increasing page speed is to use font glyphs in place of bitmap-based iconography. A custom "dingbat" font could potentially replace common icon bitmaps or even background images in some cases, with smaller-sized resolution-independent vector graphics.

Author and sustainable web expert Pete Markiewicz endorses this approach on his *Sustainable Virtual Design* blog:[2] "Since webfonts are typically just outline vector graphics, a typographic interface will have the same savings as an SVG-laden page—provided, the designer and developer optimize the downloaded font files by stripping out unneeded glyphs."

Here are some options for customizing fonts:

- FontSquirrel: www.fontsquirrel.com/tools/webfont-generator
- FontForge: http://fontforge.org/

Designing for Conversion

The interfaces where site users take actions like buying, donating, and subscribing is where the rubber hits the road: are they going to take action on your site or get too frustrated to bother? "What makes a design visible is the frustration it brings," says usability expert Jared M. Spool. "Great designs should be experienced and not seen."

Interaction designers should strive to create "invisible" interfaces, where the navigation and calls-to-action are so intuitive that they essentially become invisible to the user and thus extremely easy to use. This means that potential frustration points like forms and search functions should get the lion's share of attention from content creators, designers and developers.

Forms

Little mistakes can bring about big problems when designing site forms, so do sweat the small stuff here. A little bit of psychological insight into the mindset of your users can go a long way as well. For instance, users tend to be more apt to provide credit card information at the bottom of a form than at the top. It's a time investment thing. Also, clarity and friendliness, as well as minimizing the number of required fields in your forms will help their effectiveness. Knowing things like this will make a difference in how you design, create and test form functions. Budget an appropriate amount of time for making site forms friendly, easy to understand, and even easier to fill out. Remember, calls-to-action, which are critical components of a good content strategy, often lead to forms, where said action actually occurs so success here is extremely important.

We have discussed identifying the *one metric that matters* in past chapters. In this case that metric is likely *percentage of form submission*. If the overall number of visitors who successfully complete and submit a form is low, then you've got work to do. This is a great opportunity to do some A/B testing on form elements. If you can test which field the largest percentage of users drop off at, it is easier to make educated decisions on how best to optimize that (and other) form fields, then test improvement over time to further benchmark success.

True optimization is going to be unique for every form, but here are some suggestions for maintaining form integrity.

- Minimize number of fields whenever possible. It gets users to what they need faster and optimizes resource use.
- Give users easy access to type no matter the device they're on.
- Don't clutter forms up with extraneous design elements.
- Left align copy and fields.
- Mark required fields appropriately.
- Use informative error messages. If a form can't be submitted, clearly indicate the error and provide helper text to inform the user what to do differently.
- Use separate forms for separate functions.
- Don't return users to an altered or empty form if something is missing. Send them back to where they left off with clear labels identifying what should be changed.
- Review 508-compliance guidelines for site accessibility and then exceed them for users with disabilities.
- Test every form on a variety of devices to optimize experience.

To put some of these tips in context, let's look at two donation forms. You can instantly spot that Yale's form asks for too much extraneous information—and this screen shot is just the first page of a four-page process! However, Red Cross also has at least one field for information that's not strictly necessary to the process of donating money: an option to dedicate the gift to a loved one. Yale's form also includes this field, but look at the way the two organizations frame it.

Yale's dedication is just one field in a lengthy list; the Red Cross puts the dedication field immediately below the donation amount. This placement emphasizes the emotional weight of a donation dedication, a message supported by the image of a smiling little boy. These emotional cues tell donors that the Red Cross honors their reasons for donating and reinforces the donor's belief that their donation is meaningful and impactful. Only then does the Red Cross pass the user on to the practical details of billing information.

Search

Users need to find things quickly. Don't get in their way. Take no shortcuts on search functions. Adding easy-to-understand search capabilities that are intuitive and trackable can make a measurable difference in site and content success.

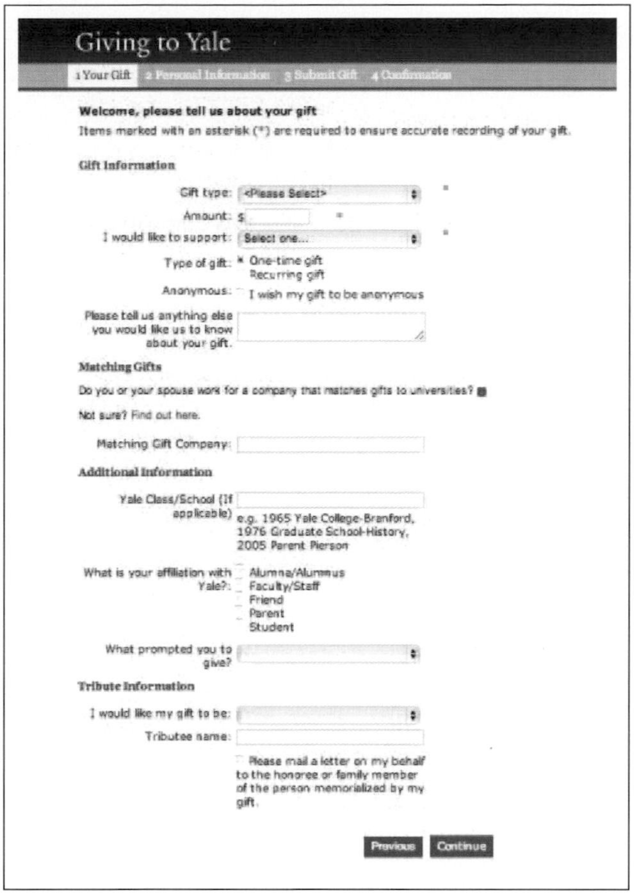

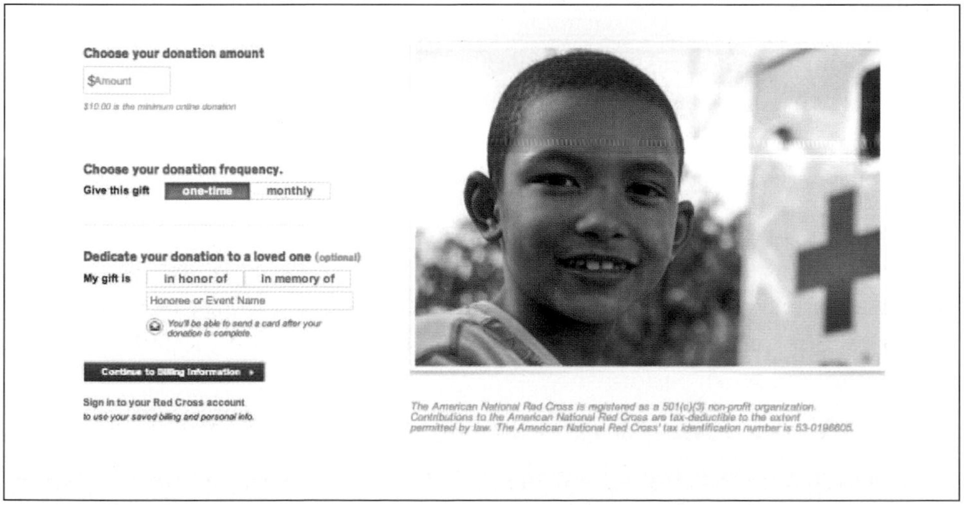

Figure 9.20 and 9.21 Donation forms for Yale and the Red Cross show the importance of good form design.

Consider the following when adding search to your site:

- Display a search box in the upper right corner of every page. (It's where most people expect it.)
- If your site has a lot of content, allow users to limit search to specific site sections before hitting submit.
- Provide search results in relevant categories (for example, product info, support, press releases, etc.)

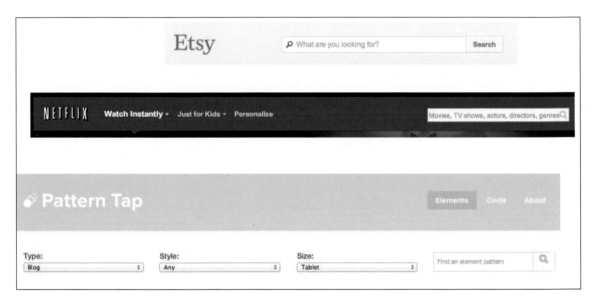

Figure 9.22, 9.23, and 9.24 Structure your search function to make it as easy as possible for your users to find what they need quickly.

Usability testing and regular prototyping during the design process can go a long way toward helping you ascertain how "invisible" your interface is.

Data-Based Visual Design

Traditionally design has been considered to be a subjective field; different people prefer different visuals and there's no way to determine which is best. But because designing for the web is designing for action, we can measure the effectiveness of design by tracking user interactions and conversions. We use the following four methods to test design performance:

1. Five-Second Test

Five-second tests help you assess what first impression your site makes on your visitors. The test is simple: you show participants an image of your home page, logo, or other design element. Then, the participant answers a set of pre-set questions aimed at discovering the meaning and messages they took away from that quick glimpse.

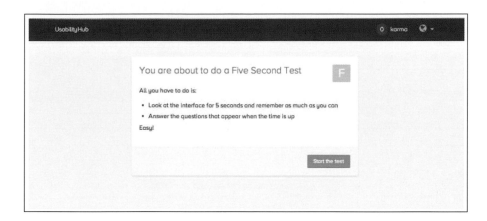

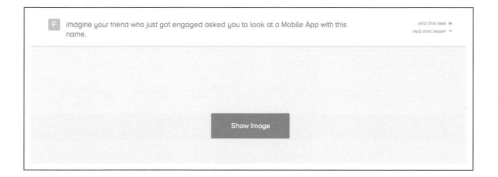

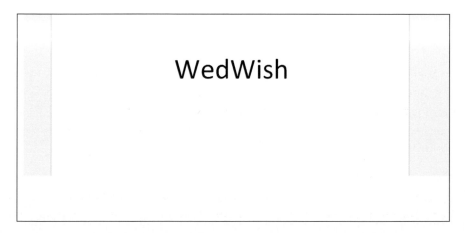

Figure 9.25–9.30 A sample Five-second test hosted by usabilityhub.com.

2. Heat Mapping

Your analytics tools tell you what links your visitors are clicking on, but heat mapping shows exactly *where* your visitors most commonly look on your page. This information can help you decide where to place your most important links.

3. Click-Tracking

Click-tracking measures engagement in your email, social media, and other marketing campaigns. Click-tracking captures not only what links get clicked in individual campaigns, it allows you to follow each visitor through to see if they converted on your campaign goal.

4. A/B or Split Testing

A/B or split testing is the practice of using a control sample to test performance on single content variables. This tactic originated in direct mail days and has migrated to the interactive world, where analytics data is used to track the effectiveness of a single site element. The most common use is generating two calls-to-action that direct visitors to a single landing page and tracking which call generates more traffic. The best call-to-action is used and then the conversion rate of the landing page is tested by creating two versions, each of which is tested for a specific period of time with the same call-to-action. Sometimes this can be as simple as a button saying "Buy Now!" versus "Download the eBook" but can generate significant results. The page that performs the most conversions is what eventually prevails. Any number of elements can be tested with this method, including form effectiveness, copy text, colors, images, and so on.

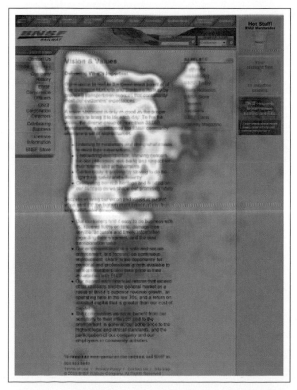

Figure 9.31 Heatmapping shows where people are most likely to look on your page. Red areas are the most looked at; blue areas are the least.

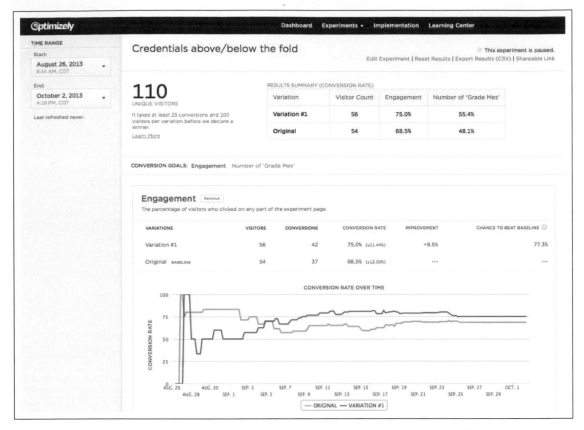

Figure 9.32 This is the result of an A/B Test we ran on our site, www.ecograder.com, to find out if we should mention that the site was in Fast Company. An A/B test showed that we got more conversions with that information displayed on screen than without.

With so many companies selling quantitative and qualitative testing as a service, it's easy as pie to get insight on your design choices. Ideally, you'd be able to test a random sample of your actual users, but even data you get by looping in your network can be hugely valuable. Here are some resources for this:

A/B Testing Tools
- Google Website Optimizer:
- Optimizely: http://optimizely.com

Click Heat-Mapping
- Crazyegg.com
- Chalkboard (Optimalworkshop.com)
- Clickdensity

Click-Tracking
- Clickmeter.com
- Mouseflow.com

Mobile User Experience

- Userzoom.com
- Perfectomobile.com

Five Second Tests

- Usabilityhub.com

Media Queries

A critical step toward designing more usable websites is support for smartphones, tablets, and other internet-enabled devices. In the first edition of this book we addressed media types, which were used by HTML4 and CSS 2 to support media-dependent stylesheets tailored for different types of media (hence the name). Creating a print stylesheet for a web page is a good example of this in practice. Unfortunately, media types didn't achieve widespread support across devices, so in CSS 3 we have *media queries*. These extend the function of media types by allowing more precise labeling of stylesheets.

Here's the W3's definition:[3]

> A media query consists of a media type and zero or more expressions that check for the conditions of particular media features. Among the *media features* that can be used in media queries are "width," "height," and "color." By using media queries, presentations can be tailored to a specific range of output devices without changing the content itself.

In other words, rather than look for a type of device, media queries look for the capabilities of that device and check for all sorts of properties, then feed the appropriately styled content to meet device criteria. From a marketing and user experience perspective, this is critical, as media queries can facilitate easier access to web content across a wider array of devices and platforms.

Conclusion

Hopefully, the topics covered in this chapter armed you with enough information to make informed decisions when designing interfaces for websites or mobile applications. Remember, well-designed, usable, and "invisible" interfaces are those that meet business and marketing goals most often, so be sure to apply these principles to your projects whenever possible.

Here's what we covered:

- How to use UX artifacts such as wireframes and prototypes to guide interface design.
- Visual design guidelines.
- Touch and mobile interface design guidelines.
- Creating invisible interfaces, particularly for goal conversion.
- Methods for optimizing page speed through design.
- Methods for testing the effectiveness of visual design.

Profile

Figure 9.33 Dan Siroker is the CEO and co-founder of Optimizely

Dan Siroker
CEO and Co-Founder Optimizely
www.optimizely.com/
A/B testing can be a great way to make informed decisions about content on your website. Dan Siroker explains what A/B testing is and how it can be useful to a business.

Dan Siroker is the CEO and Co-Founder of Optimizely, a web optimization platform that helps individuals with and without technical expertise conduct A/B and multivariate testing. The inspiration for his company came from his experience as Director of Analytics on the Obama 2008 campaign. Optimizely is a product Dan wishes he had then to make it easy for anyone to do A/B testing. Four years later, both Obama 2012 and Romney 2012 used our product during the election cycle. So have over 5,000 of Optimizely's customers such as Starbucks, Disney, and Crate&Barrel.

What is A/B testing?

A/B testing is a simple way to test changes to a website page against the current design in order to determine which design produces positive results. It's a way to validate a change ahead of time, so that you know that it will improve your conversion rate before you alter your site code.

What is the difference between A/B testing, split testing, and multivariate testing?

A/B testing is essentially synonymous with split testing. In either case, the term refers to two versions of a page, or two variations on a test. Multivariate testing, on the other hand, usually refers to testing more than two variations of a design at the same time.

Why is A/B testing important? How can it help businesses?

Improved user experience leads to higher customer conversion, higher customer retention, and improved customer satisfaction. A/B testing is an important tool for improving user experience for websites, and is critical for customer-facing websites.

Can you offer an example of cases where A/B testing made a significant difference to a business in terms of their conversion rate and sales?

One example is Electronic Arts, which ran an experiment on their ecommerce store. They are selling video games. They have a popular new game that just came out called SimCity, and in the most recent version of SimCity they had a product page that looks very similar to most ecommerce sites. It has big "buy now" button. You add SimCity to your shopping cart and you can buy it online.

When they first launched this product, they had a giant banner at the top of this website that says, "Pre-order and get $20 off on your next purchase." So EA effectively gave you a discount on your next product if you bought SimCity. That big banner at the top of this page actually moved down all the content that was necessary for you to buy—basically the "buy now" button.

They ran a simple experiment. They removed the big "Pre-order and get your $20 off on your next purchase" banner and that improved the conversion rate—the percentage of people who actually turned into customers—by 43%. They went from 5.8% conversion rate to a 10.2% conversion rate, which is a dramatic impact. What was so amazing about this is that was just by removing something from the page, not adding something. They removed a number of things that were on the page that might distract the user or a choice that would prevent them from actually finishing the entire purchase process.

Notes

1. Akamai, "Akamai Reveals 2 Seconds as the New Threshold of Acceptability for eCommerce Web Page Response Times," Sept, 14, 2009, www.akamai.com/html/about/press/releases/2009/press_091409.html.
2. Pete Markiewicz, Sustainable Virtual Design, sustainablevirtualdesign.wordpress.com/2012/12/07/html-5-api-and-other-features-relevant-to-web-sustainability/.
3. W3, June 19, 2012, www.w3.org/TR/css3-mediaqueries/.

CHAPTER TEN

Climate Ride's Pedal Power

The final leg of our journey through the twists and turns of digital marketing leads us to the story of a small, virtual organization that has used many of the techniques outlined in this book to bring about measurable marketing success.

Climate Ride offers cycling-related fundraisers in multiple locations across the United States. The organization has used digital marketing, social media and community engagement techniques to successfully drive organizational growth since their inception in 2008. In just a few short years, Climate Ride has evolved from an idea to a notable fundraising entity, raising millions of dollars in donations for national nonprofits that affect change in various areas of the environmental movement. They have done this through hard work, tenacity, and the generosity and support of their community, an impassioned group of cyclists from around the globe who believe in the vision of a sustainable future.

Climate Ride's mission is to inspire and empower citizens to work toward a new energy future. They use sport as a means to change lives and build an effective, citizen-based sustainability movement.

The organization's goals include:

- Raise money for projects and organizations that work on climate change, clean energy, active transportation, sustainable infrastructure, and public health.
- Raise the profile of renewable energy and the green economy among participants, donors, sponsors, and the general public.

Figure 10.1 Climate Ride offers several endurance-based fundraising events. The epic 320-mile California ride of 2012 ended in front of San Francisco City Hall.

- Increase awareness and understanding of the inter-connectedness of environmental issues caused by the climate crisis among participants, donors, sponsors, and the general public.
- Foster a sense of civic duty and participation that encourages engagement with members of Congress, elected officials, and national leaders.
- Promote the bicycle as a viable, carbon-free, healthy, and critical component of a green transportation infrastructure.
- Motivate individuals to take responsibility for reducing their carbon and energy footprint.
- Develop multiple events that galvanize a worldwide network of cyclists, runners, hikers, and endurance enthusiasts.

With few resources but a lot of drive and energy (the clean kind, of course), Climate Ride has been successful at accomplishing these goals and continues to set sights higher with each new accomplishment. Let's find out how they did it.

In a Nutshell: How Climate Ride Works

Figure 10.2 Climate Riders about to leave New York City bound for Washington, DC.

Climate Ride works like many other multi-day fundraising events. Cyclists sign up for a ride and pledge to raise a minimum amount of dollars before the start of the event. Climate Ride staff support registered riders with a variety of fundraising tools, webinars, training tips and online groups where cyclists can get questions answered.

While also training on their bikes for a challenging five-day ride, registrants enlist any number of fundraising techniques from social media pleas to in-person functions. Some auction off services or products they have made while others host elaborate events with bands, DJs, donated food, cocktails, and so on. As long as a cyclist has raised the minimum amount pledged by the time an event starts, he or she can participate in that event. Climate Ride is there to support them along the entire journey, from the time they sign up to the time they pick up their luggage at the end. This approach has paid off, as most riders raise well over the minimum fundraising amount.

To sign up for a ride or find out more about how to donate, visit their website at http://climateride.org

Transformative Moments: How it Started

In the latter half of the 2000's, Climate Ride co-founders Geraldine Carter and Caeli Quinn each had their own personal epiphanies about our impact on the planet and what it would mean for future generations. These epiphanies evolved into what would become Climate Ride.

Figure 10.3 Climate Ride co-founders, Caeli Quinn (left) and Geraldine Carter (right) with Event Director, Blake Holiday.

Geraldine's Story

I was riding my bike in China, climbing up a hill, as a dump truck full of coal passed me, on its way to the power plant up ahead. When it passed, the exhaust from its muffler smoked me out to the point that I had to pull over and breathe some fresh air.

At the top of the hill, there was a shiny new gas station, with 64 pumps, each with a brown paper lunch bag over its handle—waiting, in preparation for half a billion new cars to join the roads.

It was then I knew I wanted to do something. When I got back to the U.S., I met up with Caeli, and we talked about the idea that would soon come to be known as Climate Ride—and decided to try to make it happen.

Caeli's Story

I think the epiphany that led to Climate Ride was the culmination of years of traveling—of moving in and out of the "developed" and "developing" worlds and seeing everything at the slow pace of a bicycle. I grew up in Florida, unknowingly a part of car culture, where biking for transportation or recreation was simply not safe. I didn't really ride bikes until after college when I began traveling. Becoming a bicyclist changed me to the core: I became more engaged by seeing real life up close, rather than passing by at 60 miles per hour. I couldn't "un-see" life—the poverty, environmental degradation, extraordinary beauty, kindness and suffering were all there. Throughout my travels, I saw that the bicycle is a powerful tool for change. One bicycle can lift a family in a developing country out of poverty. A bicycle ride can change the perspective of wealthy people so that they see the world differently, more slowly: so they might be motivated to use their resources to help, to solve a problem, or to live sustainably. I knew I would do something that involved bikes, I just didn't know what.

Like Geraldine, in 2006–2007 I bicycled through China and Burma, where I was astounded by the rapid industrialization and pollution. Coincidentally, I settled down in Montana near Glacier National Park as scientists were exposing the effects of climate change on the park's unique ecosystem. I guided hiking trips in Glacier and quickly saw the signature of climate change all over the park. I started to see that climate change is the issue connecting everything—transportation, economics, environment, and more. When I re-connected with Geraldine—who I had met while leading bike tours in Chile and Argentina—we were really concerned about the global impacts of unsustainable practices and decided to use our particular skill set to launch a charitable bike ride for climate and environment, which had never been done. Together we founded Climate Ride and within six months organized 113 people to ride 300 miles from NYC to Washington, DC on the inaugural ride.

After a successful first ride in 2008, Caeli and Geraldine organized the New York City to Washington, DC ride again in 2009 with the help of Events Director Blake Holiday. In 2010, Climate Ride launched a second 320-mile event down the northern California coast, which they repeated annually along with the first ride. In 2013 the organization announced several new events:

- Climate Hike, a five-day hike through Glacier National Park.
- A new four-day route for the California Ride.
- Climate Challenge, a series of independent events that raise funds for Climate Ride beneficiaries as well as the organization itself.
- Climate Ride Midwest, a four-day ride through the center of the United States.

Digital tools, meticulous attention to details, and the unwavering support of an impassioned community have in several short years turned a single idea into a fundraising powerhouse that organizes events around the country.

Building Community: The Climate Ride Experience

Figure 10.4 Community on two wheels: Climate Riders connect around the common cause of saving our planet while biking through spectacular scenery, such as Avenue of the Giants in the redwood forests of California.

Before we have any discussion about their digital marketing efforts, we should first talk a bit about the Climate Ride experience overall. Engaging their community of riders, donors and supporters is a critical part of seeing strategic success with few resources, so Climate Ride puts an exhaustive amount of effort into building community through the ride experience itself.

These events inspire action and the people who put them on create transformative experiences for all involved, from volunteer crew to riders, from donors to sponsors and beneficiaries. It's the gold standard of real-world UX, with every customer service detail given the perfect amount of attention.

For some participants, these are life-changing events. Riders walk away from a Climate Ride sore and exhausted, their bodies pushed to the brink. Mentally, however, they are galvanized to play a bigger role in the fight for our environment, exhilarated to have accomplished a physical feat they may not have been certain they could pull off, and thrilled to be part of a tightly knit community working hard toward something larger.

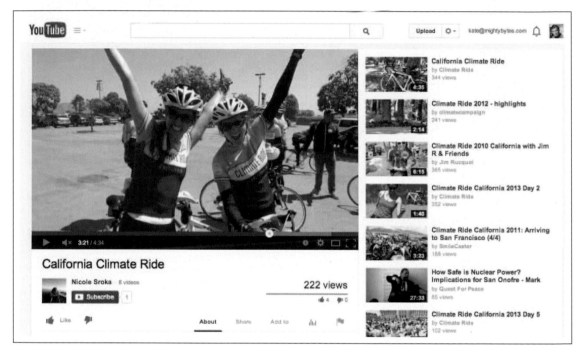

Figure 10.5 Cyclists Nicole Sroka and Katie Parker capture the spirit of the California Climate Ride in their YouTube video at http://youtu.be/jTw6oGhu7lw

"This Climate Ride was more than just 320 miles and five days . . . biking outdoors feeds the need to protect the environment," said California 2013 rider Nicole Sroka and Katie Parker in a video on Nicole's YouTube channel. "You gain a sense of appreciation by taking in nature while on a bike. It was such a fun, togetherness-type experience that I couldn't wait to hear what everybody does and how passionate everybody is, whether in their life or in their job, about sustainability."

Because of this passion inherent to both the cause and the events, Climate Ride generates many repeat riders and offers to volunteer on future events. Long-term friendships are generated between riders and, more than anything, the transformative nature of the ride experience inspires an ongoing desire to *share*: to share the ride experience, the physical challenge, and most of all, the cause to bring more attention to climate change and a sustainable, clean energy future.

"Climate Riders feel a great sense of accomplishment for having ridden their bikes 300 miles," Geraldine says. "Add to that the fact that riders often raise more than $5,000 for their favorite organizations, which is no small feat! Add to that experience of walking into your Senator's office and letting them know that you care enough about the planet to have ridden your bike from New York City to tell them—it's a recipe for a life-changing experience."

Understanding this, the organization knows they have an army of brand evangelists and *superfans* who are more than willing to help spread the word. Most times, Climate Ride doesn't even have to ask.

"Participating in the ride itself is full of amazing stories," Caeli says. "We always encourage riders to leverage their favorite social media outlets to tell their story and they are more than happy to oblige. This year we added a photo scavenger hunt, where riders capture and collect pictures of 10 specific items, then post them to Instagram using hashtag #climateride. Riders benefit because it's fun to share photos and compete for prizes. Climate Ride benefits because use of the hashtag allows us to generate photo albums and find ride-related content across multiple social networks."

This is just one of the many great ways Climate Ride and its community play mutually beneficial roles in each other's success.

Strategy: Digital from the Start

Digital tools allowed this small virtual organization to grow quickly, so building a strategy around using these tools for marketing and community outreach was a necessity right from the start. "We didn't have a lot of resources to kick off the first ride," says Caeli. "Social networks and other online tools offered cost-effective ways to build community and engage potential riders from around the country as we were getting started. We have grown and evolved our approach over time, but the central goals remain the same."

Resources

As we discussed in the early chapters of this book, digital strategy is directly proportional to the resources you have to accomplish tasks. Climate Ride's resources—like those of many young organizations similar in size—are constrained. They must balance the sanity of their small staff, who are spread across the country in different locations, with the needs of an organization in growth mode. Event logistics sometimes trump marketing tasks, but they do what they can with the resources they have. Despite the occasional necessity of marketing taking the back burner to more pressing logistics issues, they have done quite well with their limited resources.

"Social media was custom-made for an organization like Climate Ride," Geraldine says. "We couldn't have grown the organization without it. Online marketing tools allowed us to grow without the luxury of a large marketing budget. Using Facebook,

Google Groups, and other online tools we were able to make larger impact with fewer resources."

"We are also committed to keeping our overhead as low as we can," Caeli agrees. "We want as much of the money raised as possible to go directly to the beneficiaries we work with to maximize impact. Digital tools allow us to keep overhead low while still reaching our constituents in meaningful ways."

During the inevitable lulls between events, the Climate Ride staff share online marketing duties, but as each event draws near, they ramp up their efforts, oftentimes relying on their community of avid supporters and dedicated volunteers to capture the essence of the ride in a more journalistic way.

Sponsors

Climate Ride also depends on sponsors and strategic partnerships to meet the needs of tired and hungry riders as well as financial and logistical components of the events themselves. Conscious companies like Clif, New Belgium, and many others provide products that serve a wide range of event needs, from fundraising prizes to food and beverage choices at ride pitstops. The organization has received financial sponsorship from Brita as well.

These sponsors and donors get shout-outs during the event speaker series each night as well as through Climate Ride's digital channels, such as email marketing campaigns, Pinterest boards, Google+ pages, Facebook, Twitter, and so on. Sponsor mentions are a very important part of Climate Ride's digital strategy.

Strategic Partnerships

Riders and sponsors aren't the only strategic relationships Climate Ride builds. The organization has 60+ beneficiary organizations, which vary in mission from protecting natural resources and lobbying for clean energy legislation to bicycle advocacy, public health and triple-bottom-line sustainable business practices. Climate Ride's success in turn contributes to each organization's success financially, so they work hard together to ensure event success. These beneficiaries work with Climate Ride to build teams, sponsor meet-n-greet events, provide fundraising support, and many other things. Climate Ride provides each organization with guidelines for reaching their member bases through email marketing as well as tools for helping beneficiaries build teams and raise funds. This is an ongoing effort that takes place all year long.

As with any good nonprofit, nurturing strategic board member relationships plays a critical part in Climate Ride's growth strategy and it is here where we will discuss many of the digital components that make up the organization's online success. In 2011, Climate Ride partnered with our firm, Mightybytes, to transform their proprietary, difficult-to-use website into something that would work better for online marketing purposes. Shortly after the website overhaul was completed, we tackled content and social media strategy. Here's what went down.

Transforming a Website

The first Climate Ride website did its job well enough, but without an easy-to-use content management system there was only so much the organization could accomplish. They used many social tools (more on that later in this chapter), but their own virtual "home-base" was challenging to use and didn't offer the flexibility of standard content management systems for up-to-the-minute publishing.

Figure 10.6 The Climate Ride website: before and after redesign.

Website Strategy

The site's existing content management system (CMS) was custom and not very user-friendly. Its feature set was also very limiting. This proved continuously challenging for Climate Ride's small, time-constrained team. With limited staff time to devote to content and marketing tasks, Climate Ride wanted the site's CMS to be easy to use for users on the admin side as well as for potential riders, donors, and other key stakeholders.

Climate Ride uses DonorDrive by GlobalCloud to manage donations and rider registrations. This third-party hosted service offers a somewhat flexible feature set, but also presents several unique challenges of its own. As a hosted service, there is only so much control one has over design, mobile support, analytics, and key user experience tasks. The folks at GlobalCloud worked with Climate Ride and the Mightybytes web team to match the new site experience with that of any DonorDrive pages, as well as to resolve subdomains to their hosted service. These efforts resulted in a consistently branded experience no matter what tasks they need to accomplish on the site.

Other components of the site overhaul included new information architecture, a complete redesign, and many new features, including the ability for users to easily share content, photo feeds during ride events, and an installation of the ExpressionEngine CMS.

Site Goals

Mightybytes built the Climate Ride site with an explicit goal of capturing the transformative experience of a Climate Ride online while providing valuable information for these user groups (in order of importance):

- Prospective Riders
- Returning Riders
- Donors
- Sponsors
- Media
- Beneficiaries

The site would also be used extensively for content marketing during Climate Ride's events.

User Personas

Personas were created to capture the essence of each user type and defined their content needs as well as potential calls-to-action that might help them accomplish desired tasks on the site.

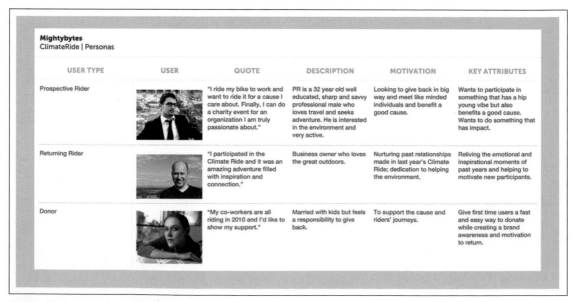

Figure 10.7 Example user personas for the Climate Ride site.

These personas were used to drive site content strategy as well as inform design decisions during the site creation and build process.

Task Analysis

Task analysis was completed shortly after user personas. Because many of the desired tasks took place within the DonorDrive registration and donation software there was only so much the team could do about streamlining those flows. Instead, a collaborative exercise took place between Mightybytes and Climate Ride to identify the following information for three key user persona types: prospective riders, returning riders, and donors.

- **Desired tasks:** what should the user accomplish?
- **Scenario mapping:** what would they potentially be looking for?
- **Influencers:** what would influence user decisions?
- **Pain points:** what might the blockers be to successfully completed tasks?
- **Desired functions:** how would the above translate to site features or functions?
- **Business goals:** how would desired tasks and associated features relate to organizational goals?

Mightybytes
ClimateRide | Task Analysis

	PROSPECTIVE RIDER	RETURNING RIDER	DONORS
TASK	Explore the CR web site and register for the ride.	Log into Climate Ride to plan for the ride. Learn about new logistics this time around.	Learn about Climate Ride and donate. Compelled by the cause. Locating the rider they want to donate to.
SCENARIO	Gain essential info with quick user friendly content and calls to action. Learn about commitment to the cause.	Monitoring and maintaing profile as well as finding site link to share for potential donors. (SEO)	Explore the website to learn the story of Climate Ride. Donate. Be compelled by the power of Climate Rider's story to increase donation.
INFLUENCERS	A story about Climate Ride that is is easy to follow and connect with. Ease of use and overall look and feel to convey vibe of the ride.	Image and video gallery of past rides. New training tips and logistics and testimonials from both rides.	Site credibility, look and feel and ease of use. Usability to cut down on time spent on the site.
PAIN POINTS	Establish a concise path to content and information about the cause and ride.	Providing archival information and changes to the ride. Being aware of changes for the upcoming ride. i.e. any things that are different than the last ride.	Understanding the cause and how to get involved. Also, if I don't know anyone riding being able to donate to "featured rider"; knowing where the $$ goes.
FUNCTION	Review content, Register.	Login gain access to information quickly and conveniently.	Successfully complete donation path.
BUSINESS GOALS	Create credibility and establish brand awareness. Easy to navigate.	Maintain credibility and energy for the cause.	Create awareness and establish branding.

Figure 10.8 Task analysis exercises were completed to identify desired goals, pain points, scenarios, and so on for three different user types.

Website Content Strategy

As mentioned previously, the overall goal for the website was to create a marketing and communications tool that facilitated easy content updates and simplified the process to register or donate. Though updates would be made throughout the year, efforts were doubled in the times leading up to, during, and just after each Climate Ride event to capitalize on the number of riders, donors, sponsors, beneficiaries and their networks focusing on ride details. As the team employed a series of volunteer bloggers and social media coordinators for each event, the amount of content created during this short period increased significantly. This increase in content and number of authors also necessitated a set of content creation guidelines. Content strategy guidelines were created based on this understanding with the intent of capturing a journalistic-style "from the road" event coverage.

Content Goals

Content on the Climate Ride website and social networks is focused on meeting three conversion funnel goals:

1. Rider Registration Funnel

Top of funnel: raise awareness to a wider audience about Climate Ride, its programs, and general environmental issues.

Middle of funnel: provide easy-to-find materials that answer questions for those considering an event (fundraising, training, inspiration, etc.).

Conversion: rider registration (individual or team).

Figure 10.9 A conversion funnel for recruiting riders.

2. Post-Conversion Rider Support Funnel

Once a rider has registered, there is also a post-conversion support funnel for riders with the content-driven tools they need to have a successful ride or event.

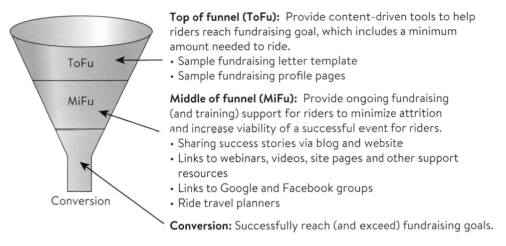

Top of funnel (ToFu): Provide content-driven tools to help riders reach fundraising goal, which includes a minimum amount needed to ride.
- Sample fundraising letter template
- Sample fundraising profile pages

Middle of funnel (MiFu): Provide ongoing fundraising (and training) support for riders to minimize attrition and increase viability of a successful event for riders.
- Sharing success stories via blog and website
- Links to webinars, videos, site pages and other support resources
- Links to Google and Facebook groups
- Ride travel planners

Conversion: Successfully reach (and exceed) fundraising goals.

Figure 10.10 A conversion funnel for supporting rider event preparation.

3. Donation Funnel

Tracking donation success offers key usability insights for both the Climate Ride website and the DonorDrive fundraising software.

Top of funnel: give riders and their friends easy tools to share fundraising initiatives with family, friends, etc.

Middle of funnel: allow potential donors to research where their funds are going through rider profile pages

Conversion: donation to individual rider or team

Figure 10.11 A conversion funnel for rider donations.

Since many of the goals within this funnel are facilitated by the third-party DonorDrive fundraising software, several measurement challenges arise, as the fundraising pages exist on a separate domain from the Climate Ride website (even though the user experience is optimized). DonorDrive allows riders to create fundraiser profiles with photos, videos, etc., and to highlight the organizations they raise money for. Tools such as content templates and fundraising tips are also provided by Climate Ride to support these efforts.

Strategies for measuring success of these efforts are covered further along in this chapter.

Content Types

To meet the needs of users defined in personas, content types that serve the key needs of stakeholders as well as content goals outlined above were identified during the discovery process. They include the following four types:

1. Written Content

Most site content exists in the form of written posts organized in the following primary categories:

- **Who We Are:** information about the organization.
- **Events:** listing of all events with descriptions.
- **About Our Events:** detailed breakdown of the Climate Ride experience.
- **Preparing:** helpful information on how to prepare and train for a Climate Ride event.
- **Fundraising:** everything you need to know about raising money for an event.
- **News & Media:** press coverage, news releases, and so on.
- **Blog:** ride coverage and targeted blog posts.
- **Store:** buy all the Climate Ride swag you can wear.

Each section above has sub-level navigation as well, as is shown by the site map in Figure 10.12.

Figure 10.12 The Climate Ride site map.

2. Photos

Climate Ride events are visually sumptuous experiences: the rolling coast of northern California, New Jersey's Atlantic Highlands, Maryland's horse country, etc. What better way to capture the beauty than through the visual medium of photography? Recognizing this opportunity, Climate Ride brings along a professional photographer on each route and encourages riders to share photos, using hashtag #climateride to help track and collect them.

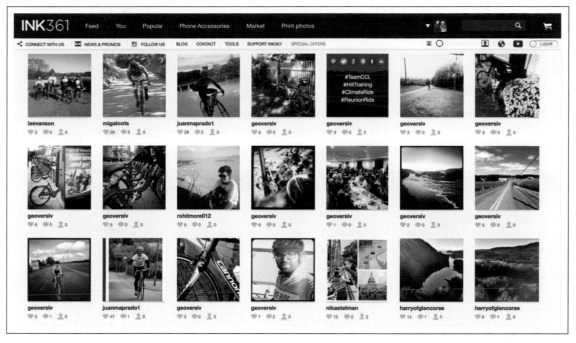

Figure 10.13 Photos play a key role in capturing the essence of a Climate Ride experience. This hashtag photo album from Ink 361 captures any Instagram photos tagged with #climateride, showing how many likes and comments each received.

Instagram photos that use the #climateride hashtag are collected on sites like ink361.com, which also offer mapping features, so donors, friends, or other Climate Ride followers can view the ride experience in pictures spread across a map of the route.

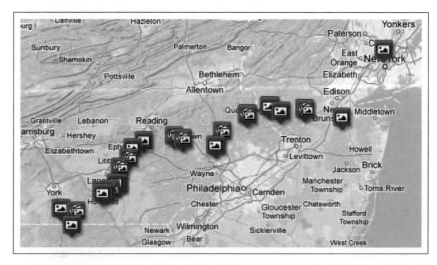

Figure 10.14 Ink 361 also offers a photo map feature, allowing donors and friends of riders to follow Climate Ride via a real-time display of photos displayed along a map of the route.

3. Homepage Banner Widget

A photo banner widget (created using SnapWidget) is added to the Climate Ride homepage for the 10 days surrounding each event. This widget pulls in any Instagram photos with the #climateride hashtag. The most recent 16 of these photos are then collected by the widget for prominent real-time display on Climate Ride's home page.

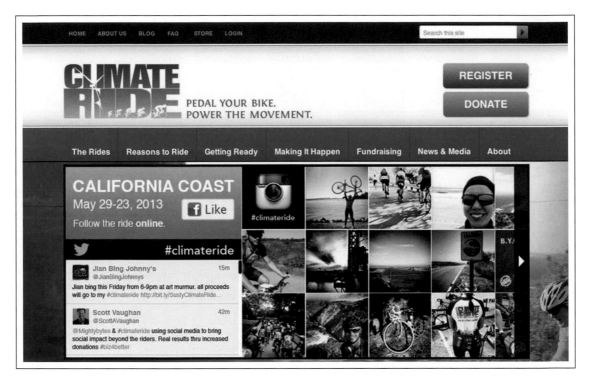

Figure 10.15 Instagram photos tagged #climateride show up in real-time on Climate Ride's home page during each ride.

4. Video Clips

Video is an engaging way to capture audience attention. It is also very bandwidth-intensive. Climate Ride endeavors to use video to capture the spirit of the ride through short interviews and panoramic b-roll of the ride experience.

Climate Ride has utilized video in many ways during past events:

- Utilizing a dedicated event videographer.
- Forging strategic partnerships with video production companies, like SmileCaster.
- Incorporating video into blog posts, email signatures, the website and other places where it might add value.

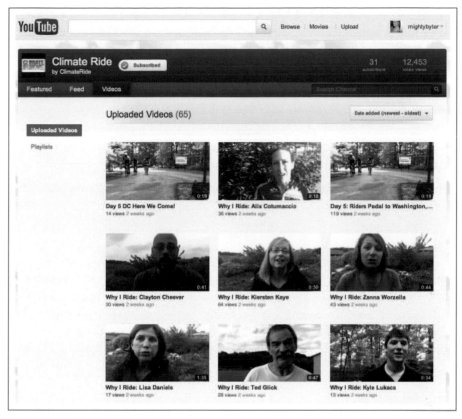

Figure 10.16 Video clips from Climate Ride events are uploaded to YouTube and shared across relevant social networks.

Content Guidelines

The following content guidelines were defined as drivers of each Climate Ride event:

- All content *adds value* to stakeholders (increases reach and "*shareability*").
- Content supports general 70/30 rule (70% adding value to readers, 30% marketing-driven).
- Create original content as much as possible. Curate when creation resources are scare to save time.
- Multiple vetted content creators will help Climate Ride share publishing efforts (board member and staff training are part of this).
- Sponsors and beneficiaries—and more importantly *the work they do*—are liberally featured. Mentions on the website and social networks are tracked and measured.
- Speakers and evening presentation sessions during any event are covered.
- Personal rider experiences are also featured.
- Content connects with real-time issues whenever possible (Keystone XL, fracking legislation, transportation funding cuts, etc.).

- Content updates also connect with *tangible results* of current or past ride efforts with predefined metrics (e.g., Beneficiary Profile: "Climate Ride was able to grant *$xx,xxx.xx* to this beneficiary in 2013 to support their efforts in *a, b,* and *c.*").
- Progress reports and daily recaps during events personalize experience.
- Guest posts from riders also personalize experience.
- Calls-to-action at end of every post (donate, register, learn more, etc.).
- Content voice is natural and conversational with proper grammar, punctuation, etc.
- Blog posts covering rides should be targeted to about 500 words each.
- Target keywords and phrases whenever possible in titles, body copy, etc.

These guidelines apply to times between as well as during Climate Ride events, though it is understood that, due to lack of resources (i.e., no volunteers), content updates will be less frequent during non-event times.

Content Governance

The following guidelines were created to help manage the content creation and marketing process throughout a given year. For the purposes of this chapter, this is not a calendar broken down by months or weeks but by post frequency guidelines. Using these guidelines one could easily transpose the recommendations herein to a calendar application. These calendar guidelines include four categories: general, pre-event, during event, and post-event.

1. General

Climate Ride engagement tends to peak during events and fall off drastically once events are over. During the times between events it is important to maintain ongoing community engagement through content (website, email, social, etc.):

- If possible, post to site at least once per week to keep content fresh.
- Post more often on social networks; engage with community regularly.
- Send email campaigns only when it makes sense; respect people's inboxes.
- Continuing weekly coverage of environmental issues across social networks.
- Regular registration discounts and other promotions.
- Cover any meet-n-greet or other outreach event.
- Highlight beneficiary and sponsor accomplishments as they arise.
- Create regular rider and team profile posts for upcoming events.

2. Pre-Event

The following guidelines are presented and discussed in the months leading up to each event. Four to six weeks before each event, content updates should be created, published and shared in a way that showcases the following:

- Beneficiary profiles: what does the money go toward?
- "Why I Ride": current and past rider profiles.

- Sponsor profiles: celebrating those who help make the events happen.
- Staff interviews: why this is a meaningful experience.
- Preparation: custom fundraising ideas, training tips, what to pack, etc.
- Resources: equipment resources, travel discounts, preferred accommodations, etc.
- Current events: breakdown of current "hot button" environmental issues.
- Sustainability: how Climate Ride keeps its events carbon neutral.

Riders are also encouraged long before an event starts to share content that may help with fundraising and to raise awareness of the ride and its cause.

3. During Event

Event-specific coverage starts as soon as staff and crew arrive onsite and continue through breakdown after everyone is gone. Specific daily content updates include the following whenever possible:

- Short written ride updates based on daily stops (profile water stops, lunch spots, other points of interest, including supportive retailers along the route).
- One daily recap of the ride experience that includes photos.
- One guest post or rider profile.
- One post on speaking/education component of each evening: what was learned, key stats, link to SlideShare of presentation deck, if possible.
- Video clips: "Why I Ride" and other coverage.
- Photos and links shared to social networks.

4. Post-Event

Because of the vast amount of content created during each Climate Ride, a wealth of content can be repurposed during times between events. Post-event coverage shows riders, donors, sponsors, etc., what the experience was like, what their money went to, and how transformative it was. Keeping the general guidelines of posting at least once per week in mind, content recommendations include:

- Preliminary numbers when possible (amount raised, etc.).
- General fun shareable event stats (miles ridden, energy bars eaten, number of sunny days, flat tires, etc.).
- Event coverage in media.
- Stats on next event(s) with links to register.
- Short rider interviews.
- Staff/volunteer interviews.
- More photo updates.

Regular site/social updates keep a continuous flow of traffic and give riders easy tools to share their experiences with donors and other potential riders. As mentioned above, content created for each ride can also be repurposed in preparation for upcoming rides.

Website UX

With such a content-intensive site, it made sense for content and design teams to work as closely as possible to ensure a seamless and intuitive user experience. Keeping navigation intuitive, content easy-to-find, and tasks simple to accomplish while still striving for a visual aesthetic that reflects Climate Ride's epic beauty remained priorities throughout the entire site redesign for all project stakeholders.

Information Architecture

With so much information targeted at so many different stakeholders, a significant challenge during the discovery process of redesigning Climate Ride's website became how best to organize site content into categories that made sense for each user group. This occurred during several intensive face-to-face working sessions with all stakeholders in Chicago.

Figure 10.17 Card-sorting exercises like the one pictured here helped keep Climate Ride site information and user needs aligned.

For this process, Mightybytes used a modified variation of the agile user story mapping process to prioritize tasks and organize content.

Wireframes, Paper Prototypes, etc.

Another primary UX challenge for redesigning the Climate Ride website was streamlining the rider registration and donation processes.

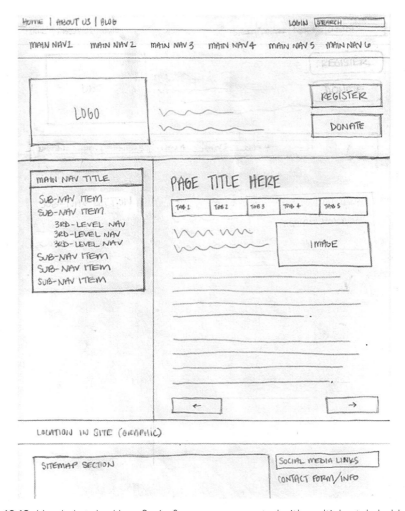

Figure 10.18 Hand-sketched low-fi wireframes were created with multiple stakeholders in the room.

User testing of paper prototypes was completed with a small group of sample stakeholders

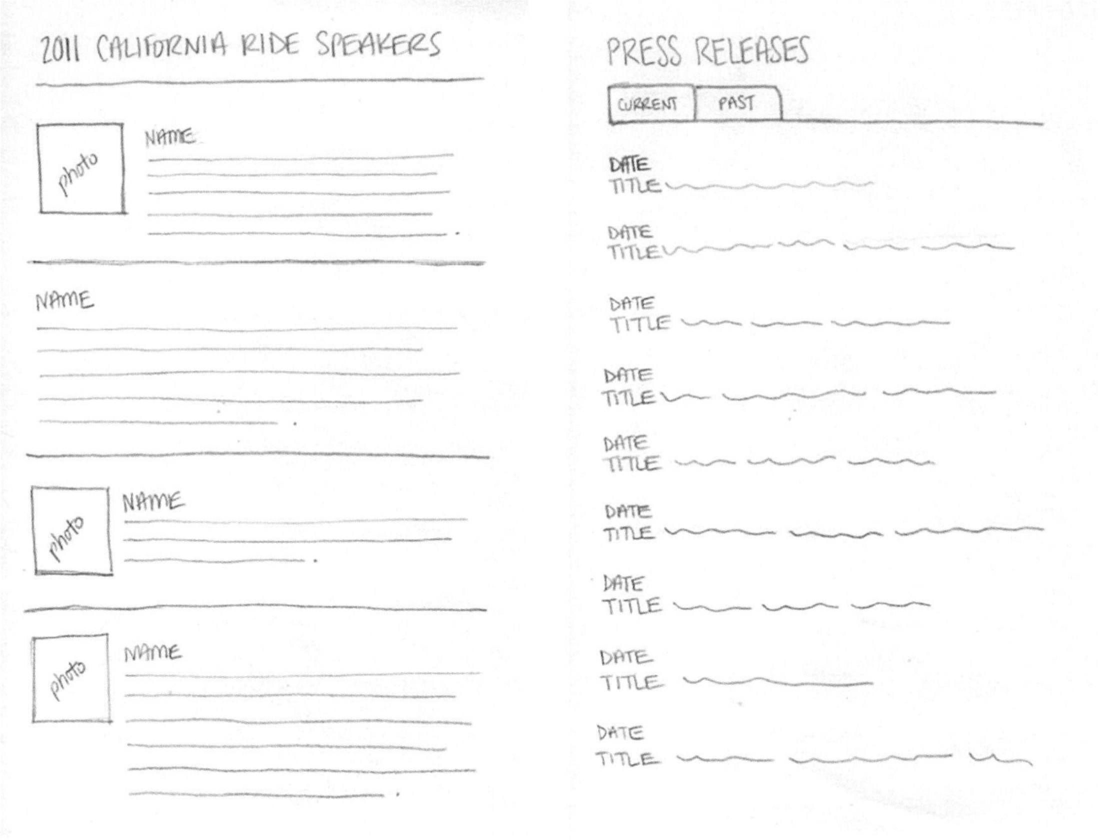

Figure 10.19 Low-fi wireframes of specific content types were presented to users who were then asked to walk facilitators through steps they would take to accomplish a certain task.

Mobile

Because the Climate Ride website uses a hosted third-party system for donations and event registration, support for a unified mobile device experience took an extensive amount of time. Thus, it was impossible to take a Mobile First approach to Climate Ride's website overhaul, as the mobile user experience would shift drastically between pages housed in the CMS and those in the third-party donation and registration system. Still, the fact that mobile support would be forthcoming informed many decisions in the design process with the goal being to streamline creation of a responsive site design when it did eventually occur.

Email Content Strategy

In 2011, Climate Ride became a recipient of the annual Emma 25 Awards, which garnered them a free lifetime account with the Portland-base email marketing software company. Access to Emma's design and analytics tools simplifies the process of designing campaigns (via templates) and offers meaningful insights for measuring success rates. With an email database of nearly 25,000 recipients, cost was a driving force in the organization's approach to email campaigns, which enforced a very judicious approach to campaign creation.

With Emma part of the email marketing equation and cost no longer an issue, Climate Ride was able to successfully integrate email marketing with their website content strategy. This gave them a chance to significantly improve content performance and measure results. Templates, like those shown below, allowed for quicker creation of email content to each of Climate Ride's constituent groups. Emma's measurement tools allowed the Climate Ride team to measure open rates, click-through rates, and many other metrics as well.

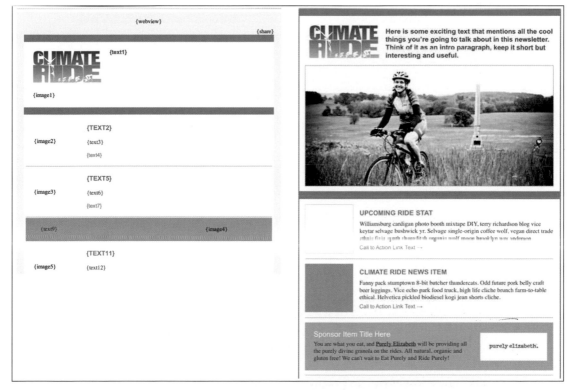

Figure 10.20 Custom templates that matched Climate Ride's branding were created and uploaded to Emma's design tools for easy campaign creation.

Campaign Content Strategy

Email campaign content reflects overall content strategy best practices in that, with rare exceptions, email content exists to support click-throughs to existing web-based content. While the delivery mechanism is different, the overarching content strategy still applies. In other words, whenever possible, Climate Ride attempts to maintain consistency across touch points for special promotion codes, specific fundraising campaigns, and so on. The emails sent out all link to site pages with more information and specific goal-driven actions.

Thus, timing for email campaign content objectives reflects that of key benchmarks for web content performance. All campaigns also include calls-to-action that support overall content objectives.

Campaign Measurement

Figure 10.21 Emma software offers access to many campaign analytics, some of which are shown in this dashboard.

Like any good email campaign software, Emma offers measurement insights for each campaign that include the following metrics:

- Bounce rate
- Open rate

- Click-through rate for each link.
- Number of unsubscribes

Email campaign click-throughs can also be tracked via Universal Analytics as well, giving Climate Ride a "round-trip" idea of how specific pieces of content perform in email vs. via the web. This gives users the ability to track campaign performance over time, repeat what works, and do less of what doesn't.

Audience Segmentation

The Climate Ride email database consists of nearly 25,000 past riders, donors, sponsors, beneficiaries, etc. These groups are segmented in the Emma software so targeted custom campaigns include information that will most resonate with recipients.

This list is segmented based on many criteria, including:

- Recipient type: rider, donor, sponsor, beneficiary, etc.
- Event location and year: i.e., California Climate Ride 2014, etc.

Figure 10.22 Campaign content click-throughs can be saved as unique groups in Emma, allowing for further audience segmentation.

Emma also features tools for saving click-throughs as groups for further audience segmentation. This way, if Climate Ride runs a particularly successful campaign, users who clicked through to specific types of web content can be saved as a group and similar content shared with them in future mailings.

Bike-Based Field Reporting

Climate Ride grew up in the era of blogging and social media, so the organization has featured online event coverage since its early days. To put their new website to the test they ran an aggressive content and social media campaign for the 2012 New York City-to-Washington, DC ride.

The primary differences between the 2012 east coast ride and others included:

- Content team of five: three on the ride and two working remotely.
  - Three "reporters" on the ride concentrated on event coverage using more traditional journalism techniques (video interviews, written stories, photos, etc.).

> One rode every mile by bike while two others set up shop at pitstops and lunch spots to collect, create, and distribute the most compelling content.
> ○ Two remote content creators tracked mentions, coverage, social sharing, and provided ongoing content for riders to share with their donors, friends and family.

- Content was crowdsourced to riders via in-person announcements during the event and easy ways to share via social channels.
- Evergreen content like rider and beneficiary profiles was created ahead of time, then auto-published (scheduled via blog) and auto-shared at specific times (via Hootsuite).
- Mobile tools such as Instagram and Foursquare were used for the first time as part of the ride's campaign.
- Climate Ride's presence was also expanded to new social networks, such as Pinterest and Google+.
- Ride coverage focused more on quick, simple videos rather than lengthy written posts.
- Used hashtag #climateride across multiple networks (not just Twitter).
- Showcased crew as well as riders in content.
- Scheduled mentions of sponsors, in-kind donors, and beneficiaries, then tracked those mentions for the purpose of reporting.

Social Networks Targeted

Content was shared by the team above to the following networks during Climate Ride NYC-DC 2012:

- Twitter
- Facebook
- Pinterest
- Foursquare
- Google+
- YouTube

Analytics and Measurement

As an event-driven organization with several events per year, Climate Ride's analytics understandably look like a series of peaks and valleys. Much effort goes into planning, supporting and marketing each event, so it stands to reason that the metrics would reflect that. Nonetheless, it is worth noting that in the ongoing efforts to continuously improve the organization's content marketing performance, this would be considered a key area to work toward improving.

With limited staff and resources, it is an ongoing challenge to maintain community engagement between rides. This small organization must iteratively:

- Balance event logistics with content marketing needs.
- Identify resources between events that can be put to evening out the peaks and valleys.
- Use and revisit benchmark metrics to inform content marketing decisions.
- Track goals and funnels for donations and registrations from event-to-event to identify areas of improvement.

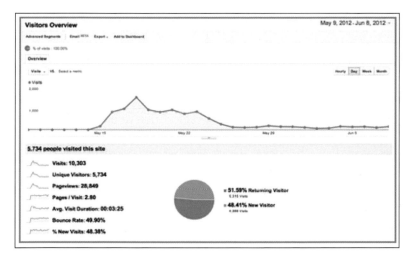

Figure 10.23 Because of the event-driven nature of Climate Ride's digital marketing efforts, their site's analytics result in predictable peaks and valleys, as shown here.

Since Climate Ride uses hosted service DonorDrive to facilitate ride registrations and donations, tracking donation success became a significant challenge.

Cross-Domain Metrics Tracking for Climate Ride

Web metrics packages like Universal Analytics provide incredibly valuable website performance insights, but when websites use third-party services for mission-essential tasks like donations, ticketing, event management and so on, tracking meaningful interactions quickly becomes a dead-end. If you're trying to track the relationship between successfully executed donations and number of clicks on the home page "donate" button, for instance, basic analytics tracking stops the second a click takes you off the primary domain. This is a problem.

Analytics apps have ways around this, however. To get a more accurate view of whether successful key website tasks are being executed successfully or not, you can use cross-domain tracking, a handshake-like method of passing tracking data from one domain to another.

Not all third-party systems for ticketing, e-commerce, donations, and so on are willing to offer this level of customization, as it requires access to key interface components on both domains. However, for those that do, cross-domain tracking used in tandem with goals and funnels can provide valuable information to help you make informed business decisions, such as:

- Did this year's investment in our website provide a tangible, measurable return on the efforts we put into it? (Might as well start with the big question)
- Should we run that holiday email marketing campaign again this year?
- Are our social media campaigns resulting in sign-ups or purchases?
- How many people downloaded a support guide, fact sheet, etc.?
- Does the "buy tickets" link on our home page drive a worthy amount of purchases?
- Were forms abandoned during the event registration or purchasing process?

In the case of Climate Ride, though the DonorDrive donation and registration pages exist on another domain, the browser resolves that domain to a subdomain of the site (bike.climateride.org), providing a seamless user experience. Even though the actual pages exist on DonorDrive's domain, they are skinned to look like those of the Climate Ride site. Thus, to track Universal Analytics funnel progress, the steps of the funnel exist on the two domains, a data handshake is required.

Here are the steps followed for getting this configured on Climate Ride's website. The nitty gritty details (and code snippets) are available via the Universal Analytics support pages.

1. **Implement Custom Tracking Codes:** Set up custom tracking codes on all relevant pages of both domains. This will allow Google to track domain-to-domain traffic as a single visit.
2. **Create Cross-Domain Links:** Add the GA custom code to any link that leads from one domain to the other. This includes buttons, hypertext, etc.
3. Customize Forms: If any of these pages use forms (and let's face it, have you seen a registration, donation, or e-commerce solution that doesn't?), you will need to configure custom code on each form's submit button (or whenever the form uses GET or POST methods).
4. Show Your Domain Names: By default, Google only shows path and page name when generating reports. To view the effectiveness of cross-domain tracking, consider customizing reports to show full domain names by creating an "advanced

filter." This will alleviate confusion when generating reports, especially if the two domain names are similar in nature.

Once the cross-domain tracking was set up and Climate Ride had the ability to generate easy-to-understand reports, they could start measuring funnel progress over time and make informed decisions about those task flows.

In some cases, the fixes will be out of your control if the usability issues are on the end of the third-party system, but at least you can approach the software vendor armed with tangible data for why they should improve their system (or lose you as a customer).

Site Metrics

During the week of the 2012 NYC-DC ride, 5,321 people visited the site. To put this into perspective, if Climate Ride were to run a Google AdWords campaign for a popular term related to their cause such as "climate change," which costs on average about $1.00 per click, the campaign to drive an equal amount of traffic to the Climate Ride site would have cost over $5,000.00. Other stats:

- Nearly 1,500 site visitors came from Facebook (web and mobile app).
- About 200 visitors came from Twitter.
- Nearly 2,000 visitors came from organic Google searches.
- Email campaign the week of the ride sent 65 visitors to the site.
- Over 50% of site users accessed the site from mobile devices.
- Site content was shared to other networks 46 times using content sharing tools embedded into the site.
- Top shared URLs were the index page, the blog, and the page with information on the end-of-ride rally.
- Funnel conversion rate for donations in the weeks leading up to and during the ride was nearly 75%.

Social Networks

Much work was done on social networks to prep for the event. Tasks ranging from Foursquare list and Pinterest board creation to connecting Climate Ride to all relevant organizations and riders across multiple networks took place before the event began. This ensured that the audience for content updates during the ride was one that would find Climate Ride's updates relevant and worth sharing.

Social Metrics Tools

Metrics and mentions during the ride were tracked via tools such as Hootsuite, Sprout Social, Google Alerts, TweetCharts, TweetReach, and others.

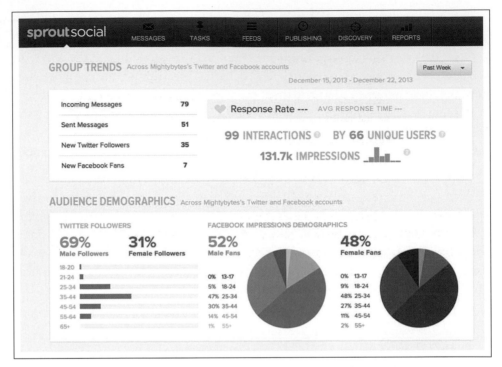

Figure 10.24 Chicago company Sprout Social was used to track many social metrics during the ride. Their software greets you with easy-to-understand dashboards for key social network accounts, like the one above.

Mentions

Here's how mention tracking broke down:

- Mentions of Climate Ride on Facebook were tracked via Facebook Insights.
- Mentions of Climate Ride (about two dozen) on other blogs, websites, and forums during the ride were tracked via Google Alerts.
- Hashtag use and mentions were tracked via various networks: Pinterest, YouTube, Twitter, etc.

Tools like Sprout Social provided easy-to-understand reports that helped event organizers better know the audience that was sharing their content. While impressions are often considered a vanity metric, in this case they were used as a tool to help organizers understand potential with the clear caveat that potential audience does not reflect actual audience.

Sponsor and In-Kind Donor Mentions

In general, donors and sponsors were mentioned 1–2 times per day during the ride, primarily on Facebook, Twitter, and Pinterest. These mentions were tracked in a spreadsheet and shared with each party.

Twitter

Twitter updates—many with photos—were made about a dozen times per day on average. The aforementioned mentions were included in these updates, as was information on specific riders, beneficiaries, "Why I Ride" videos, links to blog posts, etc. Climate Ride does not have a very active Twitter account, so the stats below reflect this.

Here are some stats on Climate Ride's Twitter usage the month of the ride:

- @climateride earned 81 new followers and was mentioned 210 times in May.
- @climateride followed 214 new Twitter users, many of them riders, donors, and sponsors who were already following us.
- Climate Ride content was retweeted 54 times and generated 489 click-throughs, most of which took place during days of the ride.
- The engagement level was at 55% during the ride, meaning that two-way conversations with other users other than one-way messages comprised over half of the tweets.

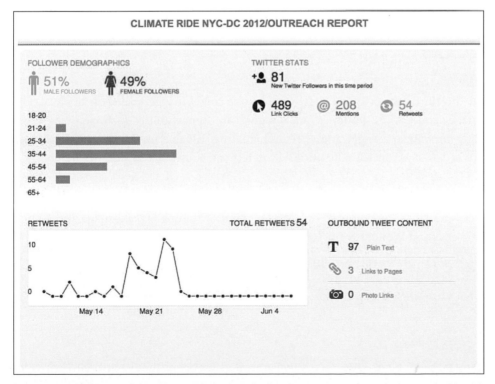

Figure 10.25a Event metrics from Twitter per Sprout Social.

Facebook

Ride coverage as well as a variety of sponsor and beneficiary shout-outs and general biking info and images were shared to Facebook during the event. In general, humorous content received far more likes and engagement than standard ride coverage. The internet likes cute kitties and stupid human tricks, what can you do?

Here are some stats on Climate Ride's Facebook usage during the month of the ride:

- During the month of the ride, Climate Ride increased its page fan base by 114 to reach 2,135 Likes. Seven people unliked the page.
- During that same time, 711 Facebook users created 950 stories that referenced or mentioned Climate Ride or shared the organization's content.
- The page had a potential audience reach of 153,125 people over the month.
- During the week of the ride, the number of people reached on Facebook averaged at just over 16,000.
- Peak page impressions occurred on May 23 at 39,105 potential users.
- Each post reached an average of 592 people.
- Facebook sends more traffic to the Climate Ride site than all the other social networks combined.

Pinterest

As the third largest social network and one focused specifically on bookmarking images and photos, Pinterest offers significant opportunities for bringing Climate Ride content to a larger audience and creating valuable online relationships. Here are some stats on Climate Ride's Pinterest account created just before the 2012 NYC-DC ride:

- Pinned 47 pieces of content.
- Content liked or repinned by notable brands, including *Outside* magazine, Climate Nexus and Wonderworld Toys.

At the time of the ride, Pinterest did not have an open API so there were not a lot of tools for tracking and measuring performance. Thus, the stats above merely reflect what was done and not as much on how it performed.

Foursquare

Climate Ride's Foursquare page was also created just before the 2012 ride. To help riders have a better experience, over 80 tips and custom locations were created in Foursquare. These tips ranged from where to find the nearest bathroom or lunch spot

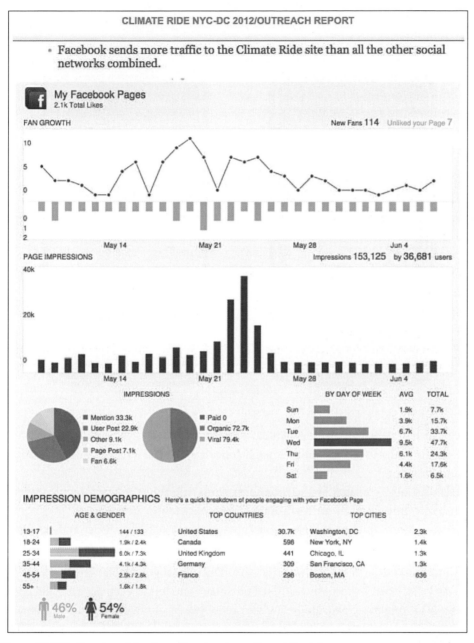

Figure 10.25b Event metrics from Facebook per Sprout Social.

to fun historical facts and location-based attractions. Tips were placed at strategic locations along the ride route. Also, if a rider got lost they could search on the nearest Climate Ride location and click "Get Directions" in Foursquare to get themselves back on track.

Here are relevant stats on Climate Ride's Foursquare account at the time of the NYC-DC 2012 ride:

Figure 10.26 One of Climate Ride's Foursquare lists for the 2012 NYC-DC event.

- Created a Foursquare list for each day of the ride.
- Each list contains Climate Ride-specific locations for water stops, lunch locations and lodging.
- Each list also contains historical information, landmarks, restaurant suggestions, and recommendations for bathrooms stops, snack stops, and so on.
- If lost, riders could easily search on Foursquare for "Climate Ride" and get directions to the nearest water or lunch stop.

Though adoption rate was low on the NYC-DC ride (about 40 followers to the list out of nearly 150 riders), those who did use Foursquare and follow each day's list said it was "*possibly the best use of Foursquare I've seen yet*" (Rider from Boston Cyclists Union).

Media

We talked about media types earlier in this chapter. Here is how those media types played out during the 2012 NYC-DC content marketing campaign.

Photos

Photos are a natural fit for sharing Climate Ride's scenic vistas and capturing the essence of the event's conservation message. Naturally, they played a significant role in content marketing efforts during the 2012 NYC-DC ride event.

Figure 10.27 One of many stunning photos taken during Climate Ride's events.

- Photos were shared to Twitter, Facebook, Flickr, and Ink361 hashtag photo albums via Instagram using the #climateride hashtag.
- Hundreds of photos were shot and shared across many social networks.
    - 189 photos to Flickr.
    - 145 photos were tagged with #climateride.
- Ink361 allowed Instagram photos tagged with #climateride (and with a device's geo-location turned on) to be displayed on a map, allowing users to view a generic map of the ride in photos.

Video

Here are some stats on video use during the 2012 NYC-DC ride.

- Shot over 60 short videos uploaded to Climate Ride YouTube channel, embedded in blog, and shared directly to social networks.
- Many riders shared these videos on their own Facebook walls, blog posts, etc.
- Channel views passed the 12,000 mark during the NYC-DC ride.

The Hashtag

The hashtag #climateride helped the team track usage across social networks that supported this functionality. Though Facebook now features hashtag support, at the time of the 2012 NYC-DC ride it did not. People use hashtags to search out groups and topics and they are supported on multiple networks, such as Twitter, Instagram, and Google+. If enough people add a specific hashtag to their tweets or status updates, it becomes a "trending topic," which can significantly increase web traffic to a particular source.

Here are some stats on the use of the #climateride hashtag (according to Topsy) during the 2012 NYC-DC event:

- The hashtag was used 561 times total.
- 419 of those were the month of the ride.
- The hashtag was added to photos a total of 182 times.
- 145 of those times were in the past 30 days.

Conclusion

Climate Ride has proven that a small organization with a lot of drive but few resources can find success with smart strategy, good content, some elbow grease, a dash of metrics, and maybe a bit of ingenuity for good measure. This chapter has shown how they put all those ingredients together to build and grow a movement of pedal-powered activism with measurable impact on climate and bicycle advocacy, clean energy, sustainability and public health. For more information or to sign up for one of their awesome events, check out their website at www.climateride.org.

Figure 10.28 Climate Ride co-founders Geraldine Carter (left) and Caeli Quinn (right).

Profiles

Climate Ride was started in 2008 by two women who wanted to make a difference in regard to climate change. Here are their thoughts about the organization in general and the role content and social media play in its growth strategy.

Caeli Quinn

What does your organization do? What value do your "customers" walk (or ride) away with?

Climate Ride is a 501(c)(3) nonprofit organization working to protect our planet and improve lives through sustainability and active transportation.

We organize life-changing charitable events that bring the innovators, entrepreneurs, and everyday people together to support more than 60 leading nonprofits working on a national and local level in environment, energy, and active transportation.

Our customers walk away with:

1. a total experience for the senses (high quality, high energy, high reward, high value)
2. the satisfaction of "giving back," a job well done
3. a new-found connection to community, to a tribe
4. a desire to engage others in that community and share the experience
5. a tangible contribution to worthwhile nonprofits

What is your primary role in the content/digital marketing efforts of Climate Ride?

As part of many responsibilities, I set the tone for communications in content/digital marketing; I write or edit most copy; I manage social media, e-newsletters, blog posts and all marketing materials. I approve all messaging and materials. I handle our public relations. Our staff is now looking more closely at keywords, Universal Analytics, and how our content serves to optimize the website pages. During the events, I monitor the social media output of our social media coordinator(s).

What is your biggest marketing challenge? How do you use content to address that challenge?

Staffing and money. I try to leverage social media and engage our participants and beneficiaries in cause marketing. We created a cause marketing platform that's fun, engaging, and promotes our community at the same time as we promote our events. We created content like a "DIY" news release so riders could engage local media to raise the profile of their participation. We have template marketing content (banner ads, text) for beneficiaries and partners to use. We leverage our board members, partners, and friends to promote our presence through social media. We create materials and content in house so we can quickly distribute it as needed.

Nonprofits often have built-in "content engines" that allow them to tell engaging stories about all the good work they do. How do you integrate that with Climate Ride's content marketing efforts?

We produce a variety of stories—rider profiles, beneficiary profiles, and route rap profiles (where we describe a day of the ride). We also have a group of key contributors who send us content that we can edit and use. This helps us tell the story of how Climate Ride affects all of our constituents and how those groups take Climate Ride back to their communities. It also helps to boost interest for those people who have not yet participated in Climate Ride—they see the stories of riders and beneficiaries enjoy and benefit from our events. Usually, we promote these stories in our e-news and social media.

If you were to impart one critical idea to a would-be content marketer about the correlation between storytelling and mission-driven organizations what would it be?

In our case, I always think about how the story relates to our constituents. It's less about "me" (the organization) and more about "them" (how they drive change and make what we do possible). I also think we do a good job of blending high-minded content (expert speakers, important news stories related to our cause) with fun content (high quality imagery that displays the fun and beauty of the events). This engages new participants and it reminds past participants of their good memories and experience with Climate Ride.

How do you blend the art of storytelling with the often technical practice of targeting keywords, optimizing pages for search engines, and so on?

This is tough for small non-profits mainly because it is less likely that you have a staff person who is knowledgeable about this. We've looked for pro-bono sources to teach us how to use keywords and optimize pages. We are a small non-profit, yet we're able to have a national presence by virtue of our website and content. I think the key to storytelling in the digital age is to keep it short, create some original content, but also draw and aggregate other great content. Also, while it is important to watch how similar groups are maintaining their online presence, I find that the best ideas come from keeping an eye on how other organizations and companies working outside of your sector are presenting information.

Does the fact that Climate Ride is an event-driven organization play into your content marketing efforts at all? If so, how?

Definitely. You'd think that because we're trying to engage people to do our events that we'd talk about our events all the time. If you were to correlate us to a for-profit company, you can think about our events as our "product." If I were to say "Our nuts & bolts are the best!" day after day, no one would care (even though they are). It's more important to talk about all of the things surrounding the events: the interesting news of the day; highlighting riders and beneficiaries, entertaining photos, science and research; ways for people to stay engaged outside of our events, etc.

What advice would you give to content creators wanting to move "beyond the blog post" to include other forms of content such as video, infographics, audio, etc.?

Videos need to be short and tell a very good story and they need to be good RIGHT off the bat. Honestly, I can tell in 5 seconds if I'm going to continue watching. Infographics (optimized to the web) are excellent to share concepts via social media, especially if they have a creative component. Audio has not been particularly useful for us as of yet.

What's your favorite technique for translating the somewhat complicated story of climate change in general and Climate Ride specifically to the "500 words or less" format of the web?

We used to talk a lot about science and climate change issues on our website. We learned that that is not the role we play and there are dozens of websites that do a great job of that. If I need to reference a lengthy discussion, I'll put it in a blog post and hyperlink to it. That way, I can keep the viewer on our website for a little longer, but then she can head to the blog post to find links to other sites. Mainly, we want to engage people in the conversation of "Okay, so these environmental issues are happening and they are serious. Now what are you going to do about it?" We have a way for you to do something that is concrete, life-changing, and actually do-able.

How do you promote your content? How do you measure the success of each promotion?

We evaluate what content draws more interest in Universal Analytics, we track what content is clicked most in our e-news. I also look at how information is digested in social media (using Facebook pages data).

Climate Ride has done a great job at building community during its events. How do you extend that idea to your blog, website, and social networks? (could include information about meet-n-greets, private social groups, etc.)

Each year, we get better and better at "capturing" the community on the ride. We create the framework and space for community and then we let things develop organically. This year we're doing a photo booth, costume day and other events that help create imagery of the community. Using apps like Instagram and Flickr allow us to quickly display that community and then re-purpose for the blog, website, and in riders' personal networks etc. That helps us to bridge the divide when we don't have the opportunity to meet potential participants in person. Quickly, they can look at our imagery and see that they would want to be a part of Climate Ride. I specifically look for imagery that gives me the feeling of 'this could be me.'

How do you measure success in your content marketing efforts? How do you improve upon that success?

My measure of success is "do we sell out our events?" We are getting closer and closer to that. It's not always easy to know exactly how a person finally decides to do a Climate Ride event (because they generally hear about it from multiple sources), but I know that our professional, fun, and inspiring content helps people to trust that they are in good hands with us.

Has analyzing your content or website performance resulted in any critical shifts in organizational thinking or a change in your approach to content marketing? If so, how?

Yes. I can see that people come to our website from a variety of sources (cycling, sustainability, advocacy, etc.). As a result, I've broadened the umbrella of our content to connect with this audience. I can see which organizations have greater success driving people to visit Climate Ride and this helps me to tailor our content marketing to specific groups. By looking at our website performance we can tell how successfully visitors and participants are able to navigate all of the information we present . . . and what's most important to them.

What is your loftiest content marketing goal for the next year or two?

Work on content marketing partnerships—with past riders, beneficiaries, and business partners. Measure if these partnerships can help Climate Ride grow. Our biggest website visitation is during the ride. I would like to see our partners leveraging Climate Ride related content at the same time as our events are happening.

a) I'd like to figure out a way to help past participants become better advocates and "content" producers for Climate Ride. Their "word of mouth" advertising about Climate Ride is our largest driver of new participants. I'd like to develop a tool kit (of content, photos, etc.) that past riders feel empowered to use to talk about Climate Ride.

b) Our beneficiaries have so much to gain by promoting their beneficiary status. I'd like to develop a streamlined system of gathering content from them and being able to re-post to our blog. Already, so many beneficiaries write amazing things about Climate Ride in their blogs—it would be great to broaden that exposure.

c) Key business partnerships—events traditionally rely upon sponsorship, but I'd like to find mutually beneficial content partnerships with key sustainable businesses.

Geraldine Carter

What does your organization do?

We organize fundraising bike events to raise awareness of climate change, renewable energy, sustainability, and active transportation.

What value do your "customers" walk (or ride) away with?

Climate Riders feel a great sense of accomplishment for having ridden their bikes 300 miles. Add to that that riders often raise more than $5000 for their favorite organizations—no small feat! Add to that experience walking in to your Senator's office and letting them know that you care enough about the planet to have ridden your bike from New York City to tell them—it's a recipe for a life-changing experience.

What is your biggest marketing challenge? How do you use content to address that challenge?

Getting the word out far and wide, to our audience. We post on Facebook and ask people to share their own experiences on our Facebook page. We encourage riders to make the most of social media during the rides, hashtagging where possible, leveraging our true believers to help get the word out.

Nonprofits often have built-in "content engines" that allow them to tell engaging stories about all the good work they do. How do you integrate that with Climate Ride's content marketing efforts?

Participating in the ride itself is full of amazing stories. We encourage riders to leverage their favorite social media outlets to tell their story. This year we're adding a photo scavenger hunt, where riders will need to capture and collect pictures of 10 specific items, post them to Instagram, #climateride.

If you were to impart one critical idea to a would-be content marketer about the correlation between storytelling and mission-driven organizations what would it be?

When people feel a genuine connection to their cause, when they feel passionately, they can't *help* but want to tell everyone. Make it easy for them, and steer them towards the channels you want them to talk on.

How do you blend the art of storytelling with the often technical practice of targeting keywords, optimizing pages for search engines, and so on?

We're not there yet, in any meaningful way.

Does the fact that Climate Ride is an event-driven organization play into your content marketing efforts at all? If so, how?

Yes—we adjust the home page of our website whenever there's an event—the home page slider becomes a feed from Instagram, and we dedicate extra resources to making sure our social media channels are posted to regularly update with fresh content.

What advice would you give to content creators wanting to move "beyond the blog post" to include other forms of content such as video, infographics, audio, etc.?

Keep it short, simple, and authentic!

Climate Ride has done a great job at building community during its events. How do you extend that idea to your blog, website, and social networks (could include information about meet-n-greets, private social groups, etc.)?

Riders continue to chatter on many different social media channels after the ride. The Facebook group sees a lot of activity—but in general riders talk in many different places, and seem to naturally meet up for official, unofficial, and impromptu gatherings of Climate Riders. The conversation is steady, and riders flow in and out of it, but they continue to engage with the event and with each other long after the ride is complete.

How do you measure success in your content marketing efforts? How do you improve upon that success?

We watch Facebook's analytics, keeping an eye on what types of posts play well, and what frequency and ratio of content type suits our audience.

We watch Universal Analytics for drivers of content to our website to determine what's an effective driver of traffic, and what's not.

Soon we'll be adding the link to our Goal page in Analytics, so that we can measure how many of our visitors from specific posts and content end up making a donation or registering.

Has analyzing your content or website performance resulted in any critical shifts in organizational thinking or a change in your approach to content marketing? If so, how?

Yes—we decided to get more systematic about posting, and have it be only one person who is the lead on social media—that way there's a flow and some continuity to posts, rather than "slap-dash," and when one person sees the whole picture and flow, they can take it in a direction better than people posting willy nilly.

What is your loftiest content marketing goal for the next year or two?

To have one staff person have dedicated time—like 10 hours a week—solely dedicated to social media, that's integrated in a Marketing role, with a strategic plan that integrates all forms of media.

Is there anything else you would like to share about Climate Ride's content marketing efforts? Lessons learned? Techniques to share? Stories to tell?

Social Media is endless and full of opportunities. However, don't let all the options overwhelm you. Start with what you think is manageable—or even a bit less—set yourself some interim goals, and get started. Measure your results periodically, and reevaluate and reset your goals if appropriate. As it gets easier and time allows, add in more channels. Keep it manageable so that it's enjoyable—if you bite off more than you can chew, you risk getting overwhelmed and doing nothing at all.

Find a person who gravitates naturally toward talking on social media. The gregarious person on your staff who already posts often (and perhaps you curse them for spending so much time on Facebook!) might be the perfect fit bolstering your social media presence.

Figure 10.29 Climate Rider and content creator Ashley Hunt-Martorano.

Ashley Hunt-Martorano
Ashley is a repeat rider and has also managed content and social media for past Climate Ride events.

What do you do?

I am the Supervisor of Program Operations for Conservation Services Group, the leader in residential energy efficiency, helping to conserve energy and make homes and buildings more comfortable, safe, durable and affordable to operate. I manage the Long Island Power Authority's (LIPA) Residential Energy Affordability Partnership program, which offers energy efficiency services for free to low income households.

In my free time I am the volunteer co-leader for the Long Island chapter of Citizens Climate Lobby, a non-profit, non-partisan grassroots organization that aims to create the political will for a stable climate and empower individuals to have breakthroughs in exercising their personal and political power.

I am originally from West Virginia and attended Marshall University majoring in Psychology. I have a Masters Degree in Clinical Psychology from Stony Brook University and have now lived on Long Island for 9 years.

How many Climate Rides have you participated in? Why do you continue to participate?

I have participated in three Climate Rides as a rider and one Climate Ride as Ride Leader Staff. I continue to participate because of the sense of community that Climate Ride generates. Meeting incredible activists and everyday citizens on the ride helps keep me motivated and inspired to keep working for sustainable solutions to climate change. I also appreciate the community that is created through fundraising. Engaging with my own network of family, friends, and coworkers before the ride to talk about the problem and solutions to climate change and request support in the form of donations creates opportunities to have frank discussions that I might otherwise not have.

In your opinion, what makes Climate Ride such a transformative experience?

Climate Ride, for me, was the gateway drug into cycling. Prior to my first Climate Ride in 2011, I had not ridden a bicycle since High School. I heard about Climate Ride through the organization where I was working at the time, and thought that it might be a way to express to my family and friends exactly how important climate change is to me. I was a self-proclaimed couch potato at that time and doing something so intensely active would really catch everyone's attention. Plus, I was coming upon a milestone birthday that year, so it seemed like a challenge which I should take on. I registered for the ride, joined a bike club, bought my first bike since childhood, did my first century, fundraised over $4,300, and completed my first Climate Ride all within a matter of only 11 weeks.

Since that initial experience, I have become an avid cyclist: I am a board member of my local cycling club, I am active in local transportation issues to advocate for safer roads, and I lead rides for new cyclists teaching them safe group riding techniques and how to ride long distances.

What advice would you have for others considering Climate Ride?

I would advise anyone considering Climate Ride to not listen to that voice of doubt in the back of your head. Whether it is the challenge of fundraising or pedaling 300 miles, if a self-proclaimed former couch potato can do it, so can you! Participating in Climate Ride will be the most transformative experience of your life and you will be surrounded by amazing people for five days on what is such a fun adventure.

What about others considering a 300 mile long bike ride?

Three hundred miles on a bike is no small feat. Go to your local, trusted bike shop to learn about local groups and clubs and join them on training rides. Getting a professional bike fit is also key. Investing in this ahead of time can help prevent problems from happening on Days 3 or 4.

What is the coolest thing, in your opinion, about helping Climate Ride with social networking efforts during an event?

The coolest part about doing social media networking during Climate Ride was engaging with the riders and hearing the many stories and reasons that people got involved. This year, more than ever, the crowd was so diverse with so many people from all walks of life.

What do you hope to accomplish through your efforts on the 2013 NYC-DC event?

I wanted to provide real-time accounts of what Climate Riders were experiencing so that the outside world could follow along and stay engaged. I also wanted to provide a story that the Climate Riders could access after the ride to remember their experience and also learn about some of the other riders who they might not have had the chance to meet during the ride. In short: I wanted to create a community.

What is your biggest marketing challenge in promoting the ride during an event? How do you use content to address that challenge?

Having participated in so many Climate Rides and having maintained my own personal blog and account of my experiences, it sometimes was a challenge to make posts seem fresh and new. I overcame this by trying to take a more personal, human interest angle to tell the story of Climate Ride. For the most part, the route and days were the same. However, the distinguishable characteristic of this ride was the new class of participants. That made finding content easy and helped the posts be new and fresh.

If there was one thing you would change about the process of promoting a Climate Ride online what would it be?

There are so many different social media platforms that it was sometimes challenging to ensure that all platforms were getting the exposure they needed to. Early on in the ride I realized that with the limited connectivity that I had and the limited time to interview riders, write content, and upload rider videos, I would have to limit some of the platforms. I chose which to post on based on the number of engaged followers. Because the Google+ page was newly established this year, there were very few followers. Also, the Pinterest page did not seem to have as much activity. Therefore, it seemed appropriate to focus first on Twitter, Facebook, YouTube, and the Climate Ride Blog and then if any time allowed after, to post to the other outlets.

Also, with the changes to Flickr's email submissions to the Flickr feed, most riders were not submitting photos. However, a huge number of riders were using Instagram and #climateride, so that seemed to be the important platform to suggest and remind riders of.

Perhaps in the future, Climate Ride should identify a priority list of applications they want promoted through, so that as the ride goes on and time becomes more limited, the social media staff can focus on the few that matter the most. There are so many platforms out there, that it's easy to become overwhelmed by too many. I know that some Climate Riders (even young ones!) were too confused by all the options and wanted to know just one or two ways they could stay engaged.

Are there any social media resources Climate Ride is not using to their fullest potential that you could see them improving upon?

Social media provides an outlet to create one-on-one relationships with individuals who are interested in your brand. I think that Climate Ride could capitalize more on this aspect of social media by directly engaging with individual users within the various platforms. For example, as people comment on Facebook posts, Climate Ride could post responses and interact with their followers. Or on Twitter, Climate Ride could aim to retweet others more often and "Favorite" or reply to tweets in which their handle is tagged. They could also retweet from others who might be of interest to Climate Ride followers (e.g., the Tour de France winner, their beneficiary organizations, well-known climate scientists).

Also, if Climate Ride could somehow provide a platform for riders to blog throughout the ride (not necessarily on the Climate Ride blog, but some kind of plug-in from outside blogs that could be populated there) or provide a list ahead of time with links to those blogging during the ride, I think it is another way that the community could stay connected with their participating friends or family and at the same time, promote the Climate Ride brand.

Index

Page numbers in **bold** refer to figures.